Best of Friends, Etc.

COOKBOOK

BY

DARLENE GLANTZ SKEES

ILLUSTRATED BY
TERRY MELVIN

Darlene Glantz Skees
804 47th Street South
Great Falls, MT 59405

Published by Darlene Glantz Skees

To order additional copies please write to the above address. Inquiries welcome concerning fundraising projects.

2nd Printing

ISBN 0-9619158-0-3

REVIEWS

A regional, non-fiction/cookbook Bestseller.
Home cookin' tops national titles.
BEST OF FRIENDS, ETC. COOKBOOK bested the famous Joy of Cooking in the ratings and also placed ahead of titles containing such famous names as Betty Crocker, Etc.
Tribune . . . T. J. Gilles 7-12-87

Best of Friends, Etc. Cookbook by Darlene G. Skees with scrumptious recipes should keep the gourmet cooks going like mad and the food processor rolling.
Reviewer Harrison Lane, for Montana Magazine Jan./Feb. 1987

Tips on preparation, complements and even the history of dishes add life to the text and a thorough index makes each recipe easy to locate. Best of Friends, Etc. in other words, is a main-course cookbook — one which could serve as the only cookbook in the house, day-in and day-out.
Bill Schneider . . . Falcon Press Publishing Co.

That Darlene Glantz Skees' cookbook Best of Friends, Etc. is attractive there's no doubt. But it's what's between the covers that counts. The book is geared to busy people who like to entertain but don't necessarily want to, or have the time to spend all day in the kitchen.
Joyce Michels, Gazette Family Living Editor

To call Best of Friends, Etc. a cookbook is a resounding understatement. There are some surprises and goodies for the best of cooks and easy to use recipes for those wanting a quick, tasty meal.
Joe Pipinich, Computer Techniques

A fun cookbook — full of whimsey and good sense about cooking gourmet meals in a simple manner.
Martin Erickson, Rural Montana Magazine

The recipes are easy to follow and Darlene's comments accompanying the recipes add interest to the book. The cookbook was designed for those who want elegant cuisine simply prepared. Best of Friends, Etc. accomplishes this.
Aurora Magazine

A 1987 State Fair Blue Ribbon and Sweepstakes winner.

About the Illustrations and the Illustrator by: Rembrandt Van Hare

Within the past year I came to live with my owner, Terry Melvin of Great Falls, Montana. She is a Fine Arts and Commercial Art graduate and former Art Teacher and Medical Artist.

Being an animal lover, she has me share my home with "Brigitte Bar-dog", the French Basset hound, and "Clive", the Silver Himalayan cat. I have been the subject of many of her studies and having the run of her garden prompted many ideas for this book. For a Dutch-Dwarf rabbit, I have a wonderful life and like to share my joys with my statuary friends.

I hope you will enjoy this book as much as I have posing for the illustrator. A daily reward of a fresh carrot is well worth the effort.

"Rembrandt"

REMBRANDT'S RHUBARB COBBLER CRISP

4 cups rhubarb, diced
½ cup water
1½ cups sugar
1 teaspoon vanilla

Put the diced rhubarb, water, and sugar in a sauce pan and bring to a boil, stirring so sugar does not burn. To this, add the vanilla. Simmer for 2 minutes and put into a 9x9 baking dish.

2 cups whole-wheat flour
1 cup rolled oats
1½ cups brown sugar,
  loosely packed
1 teaspoon salt
2 teaspoons baking powder
pinch of nutmeg
⅔ cups butter of margarine

In a mixing bowl, put the flour, brown sugar, salt, baking powder, oats and nutmeg and mix thoroughly with a fork.
Add the butter or margarine, cut into small pieces. Sprinkle the crumbs over the rhubarb mixture.

Bake for 25 to 30 minutes at 350 degrees.

BONUS: This is delicious served with a topping of honey-vanilla Haagen-Dazs ice cream.

TABLE OF CONTENTS

Page

ACKNOWLEDGEMENTS

BEV BALL
VICKI BEAMAN
RANDY BELLINGHAM
KENT BURNHAM
CAROL BUTSCH
LISETTE CARTER
JANECE CONNOR
MARGARET FARRELL
HUGH FORD
JILL FRIEDRICH
CLARA GLANTZ (MRS. JIM)
CLARA GLANTZ (MRS. RALPH)
BETTY GRANT
MARCH GRIEB
MILDRED HANSON
MARGE HERMANSON
BRENDA HICKS
GEN HUESTIS
LORA HUESTIS
JAMES KITTREDGE
POLLY KOLSTAD
KATHLEEN LORENZ
ALICE LORENTZ
CONNIE McCABE
GEN McCLURE
SHIRLEY McDONALD
SALLY McGREGOR
JUDY McINTYRE
MARY MASON
TERRY MELVIN
NANCY PANNELL
MOLLY PERSON
JANICE SAX
KARI SHAY
BEV SHERMAN
BERTIE J. SIGVARDT
HELEN SIMON
JOHN SKEES
LARUE SMITH
JEANIE RAHN STAHL
BARBARA EASTLICK STOUT
DEBBIE SULLIVAN
POLLY THISTED
MARILLYN THOMAS
BETTY USHER
BETTE WEISSMAN
DIXIE WHIPPLE
ELIZABETH YOST

MY SPECIAL THANKS TO ALL *KNOWN AND UNKNOWN FRIENDS* WHO HAVE CONTRIBUTED TO THE CREATION OF *BEST OF FRIENDS, ETC.*

I IN TURN HAVE ENDEAVORED TO FASHION A COOKBOOK FROM WHICH TRULY ELEGANT CUISINE CAN BE SIMPLISTICALLY PREPARED. *BEST OF FRIENDS, ETC.* WAS DESIGNED FOR THOSE WHO NOT ONLY ENJOY BEING ENTERTAINED BUT WHO ENJOY ENTERTAINING.

MOST OF US ARE LIMITED IN THE TIME WE CAN DONATE TO PERFECTION IN THE KITCHEN—THAT IS WHY I AM CONFIDENT YOU WILL READILY AGREE THAT *BEST OF FRIENDS, ETC.* WILL BECOME YOUR BEST FRIEND INDEED!

DARLENE GLANTZ SKEES

FOREWORD

For those of us who have had the good fortune to be invited to Darlene's table presented with gourmet dishes, we have become aware that cooking is not only an important skill, but an endeavor to achieve perfection with ease. It is her joy not only to cook but to share with everyone the uncomplicated and many times humorous creativity of her recipe writing. Darlene has collected and embellished recipes for years, having tested and written for her Junior League's contribution to "The Western Junior League Cookbook" and other regional cookbooks. Being a professional person working outside of her home, she found a need for a cookbook containing good cuisine which can be prepared easily. BEST OF FRIENDS, ETC. is the culmination of that endeavor.

Best of Friends

SAGACIOUS TIDBITS
FROM THE AUTHOR/CHEF

*There are many hints and asides throughout the formulation of **BEST OF FRIENDS, ETC.** Perhaps these subtleties will not penetrate themselves sufficiently to **coerce** you, the prospective re-creator of my collection of best of friends' truly tried and tested recipes, so I have chosen to preface the cookbook with **Sagacious Tidbits from the Author/Chef** . . Please read on—and heed . .*

1. Freshly grated nutmeg is beyond comparison, and it is utilized in many of the recipes. Scurry to the nearest cooking gadget section of most any department store, super market, or specialty cookware store and you will find a hand-held nutmeg grater for about $2.00. Believe me, it is one of the best investments you can make. You will be amazed that you ever struggled along without it.

2. When you seen an italicized word, such as *freshly squeezed orange juice,* etc., you can use bottled or prepared, but the recipe really needs that freshly squeezed orange juice to reach the peak of perfection in appearance and taste. This holds true for baked goods as well as entrees, soups, etc. Pay heed to any other *italicized* tidbits — they are helpful hints, indeed.

3. The BONUS sections of most of the recipes are truly revealing and are ideas that I have gleaned from testing and tasting all of them. I have attempted to be very specific in writing the recipes and perhaps I have gone too far back to the *basics*, but too many people do not like to cook because recipes sometimes are merely a list of ingredients and the directions leave more than lots to be desired.

4. I personally become aggravated when a recipe calls for an ingredient that is only available to those in a specific geographic area. I have endeavored to give an alternative if I feel the ingredients are foreign to areas other than where the recipe originates.

5. When an item needs to go into the oven at a certain temperature—350 degrees—the oven should be preheated—the thermometer scale is Fahrenheit.

6. With some of the Entrees, I have given examples of what I have personally served with them—a salad, dessert, wine, etc. I find planning a menu sometimes time-consuming because I can't come up with a tempting combination. I hope you will find these suggestions helpful. The *example recipes* are in *BEST OF FRIENDS, ETC.*

BON APPETIT!

APPETEASERS:

APPETEASERS:

Asparagus-Bacon Rollups - 27
Barbecued Chicken Wings - 24
Brie in a Crust - 26
Caraway Cheese Wedges - 13
Cocktail Smokies - 24
Crabmeat Mold - 19
Crab-Stuffed Phyllo - 18
Crab Swiss Bites - 16
Guacamole - 13
Ham & Chutney Turnovers - 28
Hot Crab Dip - 17
Incomparable Antipasto - 15
Jalepeno Tortilla Rolls - 16
Marinated Shrimp - 20
Mini Quiches - 21
Mushroom Pate - 23
Piquant Seafood Fare - 17
Sauerkraut & Ham Balls - 25
Spicy Cocktail Balls - 23
Stuffed Mushrooms Parmesan - 22
Stuffed Shrimp - 20
Texas Caviar - 28
Tex-Mex Taco Dip - 14

POTABLES:

Banana Zinger - 33
Brandy Alexander - 35
Brandy Slush - 32
Cappuccino - 30
Chocolate Instant Nog - 37
Coffee Mocha Nudge - 30
Coffee Nog - 36
English Toffee Freez - 31
Golden Fizz - 35
Honey, Babe - 29
Hot Mulled Cider - 31
Margaritas - 32
Peppermint Patty - 36
Ramos Fizz - 34
Slushy Daiquiris - 31
Spiked Sangria - 34
Strawberry Blush - 33
Tom & Jerry Batter - 38

CARAWAY CHEESE WEDGES

If you like caraway—this appeteaser is a pleasant delight.

2 slices lean bacon chopped
1 small onion, minced
¾ cup shredded Swiss
  cheese
3 eggs well beaten with
  3 tablespoons sour cream
½ teaspoon salt
2 dashes pepper
¼ teaspoon caraway seed

Brown the bacon, add onion and brown slightly.
Cool—add remaining ingredients.
Pour mixture in 9 inch pastry* lined pie tin.

Bake at 350 degrees for 30 minutes.

Cut into thin wedges for a great appeteaser.

*I use my basic recipe for pie crust which is included in BEST OF FRIENDS, ETC.—if you have your own favorite pastry recipe—have at it.

GUACAMOLE

4 avocados
½ cup mayonnaise
¼ cup minced onion
  (green onions are best)
1 teaspoon salt
3 tablespoons lemon juice
2 teaspoons chili powder
1 teaspoon garlic powder
½ teaspoon tabasco sauce

1 fresh tomato chopped
  for garnish

SERVE with Cheese-flavored Nacho chips, taco chips, etc.

BONUS: This guacamole can also be used in the Tex Mex Taco Dip in place of *smashed* avocados. I have frozen leftover Guacamole and used it in the Tex Mex Taco dip—give it a try.

TEX—MEX TACO DIP

*A most popular **taco-like** dip and popular with everyone including the kids— for those few who do not like avocados or black olives— skip them (the partakers or the avocados and black olives) and carry on...*

2 cans bean dip (or one can refried beans)

Spread on large round tray or plate—I use large quiche-like dish.

3 avocados "smashed"
- mixed with
2 tablespoons lemon juice
½ teaspoon salt
¼ teaspoon pepper

Spread over bean mixture.

1 cup sour cream
½ cup mayonnaise
1 package Taco seasoning
mix

Mix and spread on top of avocado mix.

Chop—1 bunch green onions—sprinkle over above mixture.

Follow with:

l or two small cans of sliced
or chopped black olives
1 cup grated sharp cheddar cheese
(New York style is good)
1—2 tomatoes cubed

Also—a small can of chopped green chilies sprinkled here and there adds a bit of *zing* to the whole thing.

SERVE WITH LARGE TACO CHIPS

BONUS: If you are lucky enough to find frozen Guacamole dip, it is better than the *smashed avocados*.

INCOMPARABLE ANTIPASTO

Incomparable Antipasto is second to none. It is delicious right out of the jar with no accompaniment but equally delectable with a wheat-thin cracker. There are no holds barred when it comes to serving this appeteaser to your family or guests.

1 head fresh cauliflower—
cut in pieces (pour boiling
water over and set aside
for 10 minutes)
2 or 3 carrots—cut in small
pieces (boil for 10 minutes)

The following drained and
cut in pieces:

1—16 ounce can green beans
1—5 ounce jar pickled onion
(cut them in half)
1—10 ounce jar *salad*
stuffed green olives
1 medium can pitted black
olives
1 small jar dill pickles
(or about three large
pickles cut up)
1 green pepper chopped
2—4 ounce cans mushroom
pieces
1 can anchovies
1—32 ounce bottle catsup
1—12 ounce bottle chili sauce
¼ cup vegetable oil
¼ cup cider vinegar
1 teaspoon salt
2 celery sticks—diced

Bring all ingredients to a boil and cook 5 minutes. Remove from heat and add one 10¾ ounce can of water packed tuna—flaked.

Spoon into hot sterilized jars and adjust lids according to manufacturer's instructions.

Process in boiling water bath (pints) 20 minutes.

Depending upon size of cauliflower, etc., you should get approximately 6 to 7 pints.

BONUS: If you do not use hot water bath to seal jars, keep refrigerated tightly covered. If stored in refrigerator, antipasto will keep for 3—6 months.

JALEPENO TORTILLA ROLLS

Terrifically spiced appeteasers befitting any cocktail hour.

6 8-inch flour tortillas
12 ounces *whipped* cream
   cheese
3 tablespoons chopped
   jalepeno peppers or
   green chilies
3 tablespooons finely
   chopped pecans
3 tablespoons chopped
   ripe olives
4½ tablespoons green
   onions, minced
Dash garlic powder

Combine the cream cheese and all other ingredients. Spread mixture over top of each tortilla—completely covering to the edges. Roll each tortilla up tightly, jelly roll style. Wrap in plastic wrap and refrigerate several hours or overnight.

To serve, cut each long roll into one-half inch rounds and lay, cut side down, on a doilie-lined serving tray. (The cook gets to test taste the ends as they are not for the serving tray).

BONUS: During the Christmas holidays, add some chopped pimento to give that red and green Christmasy touch.

CRAB SWISS BITES

*An impressive appeteaser served on a **doilie** lined serving plate!*

1—7½ ounce can crab meat,
   drained and flaked
1 tablespoon sliced
   green onion
4 ounces—Swiss cheese,
   shredded—(1 cup)
½ cup mayonnaise
1 teaspoon lemon juice
¼ teaspoon curry powder
1 package flaky style
   refrigerated rolls (12)
1—5 ounce can sliced water
   chestnuts (⅔ cup)

Combine the crab meat, green onion, Swiss cheese, mayonnaise, lemon juice and curry powder—Mix well.

Separate each roll into three layers. Place on an ungreased baking sheet, spoon on the crab meat mixture—dividing equally. Top each with water chestnuts.

Bake 400 degrees for 10 to 12 minutes

Yield: 36 Bites

PIQUANT SEAFOOD FARE

A party dip that is supreme in all respects. A blending of crab, shrimp and minced clams with veggies results in a very enticing and harmonious composition.

1—4½ ounce can crabmeat, drained
1—4½ ounce can shrimp, drained
2—4½ ounce cans minced clams, drained
1 cup chopped celery
1 cup chopped green or red pepper
1 cup stuffed green olives, halved
1 cup chopped onions
1 12-ounce bottle Seafood cocktail sauce
1 l2-ounce bottle catsup

Mix all of the above ingredients and chill overnight.

Serve with assorted crackers.

BONUS: This dip freezes well.

HOT CRAB DIP

This is an old, tried and truly yummy dip!

1—8 oz. packages of cream cheese
1 small jar dried chipped beef
1 tablespoon lemon juice
1 tablespoon Worcestershire sauce
1/8 teaspoon cayenne
1 can crab
3 tablespoons milk
1 medium onion—chopped
Paprika
Slivered Almonds

Whip the cream cheese, adding milk and lemon juice. Add remaining ingredients and place in a shallow ovenproof dish. Sprinkle with paprika and slivered almonds.

Bake at 350 degrees until hot. Serve with crackers of your choice. Wheat Thins are my favorite with this dip.

CRAB-STUFFED PHYLLO

The fun of making the crab-stuffed phyllo triangles is that you can do them ahead of time—the day before or a month before serving. They can be frozen and then popped into the oven after thawing. The phyllo triangles are also a very impressive addition to a buffet table. The triangles are fun and amazingly easy to prepare. TRY THEM!

1 tablespoon unsalted
  butter
1 tablespoon flour
½ cup milk
½ teaspoon salt

3 shallots, minced
  (use 1 tablespoon dried
  minced onion if you can't
  find shallots).
1½ tablespoons unsalted
  butter
2 cans (6½ oz.) flaked
  crabmeat (or 1 cup)
1 egg yolk lightly beaten
1 teaspoon lemon juice

¼ teaspoon freshly grated
  nutmeg*
¼ teaspoon freshly ground
  pepper (white if you
  have it)

5 sheets of phyllo (you can
  find this in frozen food
  section at grocery store)
½ cup melted unsalted
  butter

Melt 1 tablespoon butter in small saucepan; whisk in flour and cook 1 minute; whisk in the milk and cook, whisking constantly until smooth and thickened. This should take about 3 minutes. Stir in salt.

Saute shallots or minced onion in 1½ tablespoons butter in a skillet over medium heat (I use my electric frypan). On low temperature stir in the whitesauce, crab, egg yolk, lemon juice, nutmeg and pepper. Cool.

Brush 1 sheet of phyllo with melted butter, cut into six 2-inch wide strips; place about 1 teaspoon of filling in top corner of one strip; fold corner over to opposite edge and continue folding as you would a flag—keeping the triangular shape with each fold. Place on buttered baking sheet. Repeat with remaining phyllo and filling.

Bake in 400 degree oven until phyllo puffs and turns golden—about 15 minutes. Best served warm.

Yield: about 36 appeteasers.

BONUS: The phyllo triangles can be frozen before baking. I freeze on a cookie sheet; then package. Thaw and bake at 350 degrees—15 to 18 minutes.

*If you don't own a nutmeg grater, let me be the first to tell you that the investment (about $2.00) is well worth the taste and fragrance you get from freshly grated nutmeg—TRY IT - YOU'LL BE AMAZED!

CRABMEAT MOLD

*This is a favorite **appeteaser** - it can be made the day before and goes far into the night—i.e.—it makes about 48 appeteaser servings.*

1 can cream of shrimp soup, undiluted
2—3 oz. size cream cheese
¼ cup finely chopped onion
1 cup mayonnaise
2 envelopes *unflavored* gelatin
1 cup cold water
1 can crabmeat, (rinsed and drained) flaked
1 cup finely chopped celery

In medium saucepan, combine soup, cheese and the onion. Heat until cheese is melted, stirring constantly.

Blend in the mayonnaise and remove from heat.

In another small saucepan, sprinkle the gelatin over the water. On low heat, stir until gelatin dissolves. Then stir this into the soup mixture. Add the crabmeat and celery.
Pour mixture into a 6-cup mold—refrigerate at least 6 hours, or until firm. Unmold on serving plate.

BONUS: I use a fluted round mold, but if you have a Fish mold, that might be interesting—I personally do not like to dip into a *wiggly* fish with olive eyes and pimento *scales*.

MARINATED SHRIMP

1—2 pounds medium or
large cooked and shelled
shrimp
1 onion, thinly sliced
(Bermuda or Purple
are great)

Layer the shrimp and onion slices until used up—use a clear glass shallow bowl if you have one. Marinate at least overnight in the marinade.

MARINADE:

½ cup salad oil
1½ cups vinegar
(Tarragon is nice)
2½ teaspoons Capers (those
little round green things
that look like tiny green
peas—in a bottle)
2½ teaspoons celery seed
8 whole cloves
1 clove garlic minced
(or powdered garlic to
taste or neither)
1½ teaspoons salt
2 bay leaves
4 peppercorns

BONUS: These *pickled* shrimp will keep for at least a week in the refrigerator—keep well covered. Shrimp can be used as an appeteaser or on a buffet table, etc. If using for appeteaser, have toothpicks handy. This is definitely a *repeater* item.

STUFFED SHRIMP

*These are fun to prepare. If you have a **shrimp peeler** it makes the job a little easier.*

3 pounds large shrimp,
cooked, shelled and
deveined
1 package (3 oz.)
cream cheese
½ cup (3 oz.) American
blue cheese

Cook the shrimp in salted, boiling water for 3—5 minutes. Drain, and chill. Peel the shrimp before proceeding. Mix the cheeses together and gradually stir in the beer. Slit the shrimp part way along the vein side—like butterflying only don't make a full

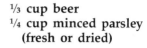
⅓ **cup beer**
¼ **cup minced parsley**
  (fresh or dried)

butterfly cut. (I do this with a small paring knife). Stuff with the cheese mixture. Roll cheese side of the stuffed shrimp in the parsley. You certainly won't need any other goodies to serve with these yummy morsels except perhaps a touch of liquid refreshment.

This makes about 4 dozen appeteasers depending on size of shrimp. You can *halve* the recipe if you don't wish to stuff all that many.

MINI QUICHES

An old standby—worth repeating—!

1 **package refrigerated**
  butterflake dinner rolls
  (12)
1—4½ **ounce can** *cocktail*
  shrimp (1 cup)—drained
1 **beaten egg**
½ **cup light cream**
  (Half & Half)
1 **tablespoon Brandy**
½ **teaspoon salt**
Twist of the pepper mill
  (or a dash of pepper)
1⅓ **ounces Gruyere cheese**
  (3 triangles)

Grease 24 miniature muffin cups (2 pans)
Separate each dinner roll in half—press into the muffin pans to make *shells* - place a few shrimp in each shell.

Combine the egg, cream, brandy, salt and pepper. Divide evenly among the shells, using about 2 teaspoons for each.
Slice the cheese into 24 small triangles—place one atop each appeteaser.

Bake in 375 degree oven for 20 minutes or until golden. Serve warm.

BONUS: The quiches freeze nicely—just cool after baking, wrap in foil and freeze. To serve—place frozen appeteasers on a baking sheet and bake at 350 degrees for 10 to 12 minutes.

STUFFED MUSHROOMS PARMESAN

A delightfully stuffed mushroom that may be used as a first course appetizer, before or after the game snack, or a light main course with a greens-type salad and a nice Burgundy wine...

12 extra-large fresh
mushrooms (24 ounces)
2 tablespoons butter
1 medium onion,
finely chopped
2 ounces diced pepperoni
(about ½ cup give or take)
¼ cup finely chopped
green pepper
A few shakes of garlic salt
(may omit)

½ cup crunched Ritz
crackers
3 tablespoons grated
parmesan cheese
(fresh would be nice)
1 tablespoon snipped fresh
parsley (I use dried)
½ teaspoon seasoned salt
¼ teaspoon dried oregano
leaves crushed
A shake of pepper
(or dash—whichever
you prefer)
⅓ cup chicken broth
(homemade or canned or
I use chicken bouillon
if I don't have broth
available)

Clean the mushrooms (wash or use mushroom brush). Remove the stems.

Finely chop the stems and reserve. Drain caps on paper toweling if you wash them. Melt butter in skillet and add:

Onion, pepperoni, green pepper, garlic salt and chopped mushroom stems. Cook until veggies are tender but not browned.

Add:

Cracker crumbs, cheese, parsley, seasoned salt, oregano, and pepper. Stir in the broth or bouillon.

Spoon stuffing into mushroom caps, rounding off the tops. Place in shallow baking pan with a scant ¼ inch of water covering bottom of pan. Bake uncovered at 325 degrees, about 25 minutes or until heated through.

SPICY COCKTAIL BALLS

¾ **pound ground beef (lean)**
1 4¾-ounce can liver spread
1 teaspoon prepared mustard
½ **teaspoon salt**
1/8 teaspoon pepper
¼ **cup fine dry breadcrumbs**
1 slightly beaten egg
2 cups corn chips crushed
(¾ cup)

COMBINE:

Ground beef, liver spread, mustard and seasonings until well blended. Add the crumbs and egg. Mix thoroughly—shape into 1 inch balls using a rounded teaspoon of meat mixture for each. Cover tightly and refrigerate overnight. Just before baking, roll in the crushed corn chips.

Bake on rack in shallow pan for 10 minutes at 350 degrees. Turn once and bake 10 minutes more.

Makes about 60 meatballs.

MUSHROOM PATÉ

This is a most elegant appeteaser—it can be served at a pre-dinner affair or a summertime picnic, pre or apre football game, etc.

1 lb. mushrooms (fresh)
½ **cube butter**
1 tablespoon lemon juice—
fresh is best
1/8 teaspoon cayennne
1 cube butter at room
temperature
2 eggs—scrambled
(in a bit of butter)
4 tablespoons parmesan
cheese—fresh is best
¼ **teaspoon tarragon vinegar**
½ **teaspoon ground pepper**
¼ **teaspoon salt**

Slice mushrooms (a food processor is great for this) . . saute in the ½ cube of butter. Cook for about 5 minutes, moving the mushrooms about in the pan frequently—wooden spoon works nicely.
Puree mushrooms and the juice in a blender or food processor. Cool. Add the rest of the seasonings and the soft cube of butter. Transfer to a bowl and add the scrambled eggs and parmesan. Mix well, put in a crock or crock-like container and refrigerate. Serve with crackers of your choice—melba rounds are good. This should make about 2 cups.

COCKTAIL SMOKIES

This is one version of the always popular cocktail weiner.

1 tablespoon corn starch
½ cup brown sugar
⅓ cup vinegar
6 tablespoons pineapple
    juice
2 teaspoons Soy sauce

Bring all ingredients to a boil and cook until thickened. Add four or five packages of Little Smokies.

Serve in a chafing dish—keep the Smokies warm for best flavor.

BARBECUED CHICKEN WINGS

This is for my dear friend Bev who likes chicken wings almost as much as oysters on the half shell...

4 pounds chicken wings
    (cut off tips and use
    for chicken broth)
1 cup brown sugar
¾ cup Soy sauce
1 cup water
¼ cup butter
1 teaspoon dry mustard
    (this is what gives the
    wings the *zing.*

Melt the butter and add remaining ingredients, except wings. Bring to boil. Pour over chicken wings which have been placed in a container single layered. Marinate overnight. Next day bake in a 350 degree oven for 45 minutes on one side, and another 45 minutes after turning the wings over. (If they aren't browned and a little crunchy, pop them under the broiler for a minute or two).

This is a very easy and delicious version of appeteaser chicken wings.

BONUS: On the right day, you might be able to find the chicken wings already prepared for this recipe so you won't have to cut the tips off yourself. I guess it depends on what mood the butcher is in on any given day.

SAUERKRAUT & HAM BALLS

Sauerkraut can be overly assertive, but in these appeteasers, it adds a savory tang and pleasant texture. They can be frozen and reheated which is a delightful bonus.

3 tablespoons butter
1 medium onion,
  finely chopped
6 tablespoons all-purpose
  flour
2 cups ground lean cooked
  ham
1 egg slightly beaten
1 can sauerkraut (1 lb.)—
  drain well and finely chop
½ teaspoon Worcestershire
  sauce
1 tablespoon chopped
  parsley (dried can be
  substituted)
Salad oil for frying

BATTER:
1⅓ cups flour
½ teaspoon paprika
1 cup water

In large frying pan melt the butter over medium heat; add onion and saute for about 5 minutes. Add the flour; cook 3 minutes. Remove from heat and stir in ham, egg, sauerkraut, Worcestershire and parsley. Blend well. Cover and chill thoroughly.

In a deep pan or deep fat fryer, heat 2 inches of oil to 375 degrees. Prepare batter, shape ham mixture into walnut-size balls. Dip each ball into batter, drain briefly and fry a few at a time in the hot oil until golden. (This should take about 2 minutes). Remove with a slotted spoon and drain on paper toweling. Arrange on a cookie sheet in single layer and freeze. Package airtight.

To serve, if frozen, heat uncovered in a 400 degree oven for 15 minutes or until heated through.

This recipe makes 4 to 5 dozen appeteasers.

BONUS: I like to serve the sauerkraut balls with a bowl of hot mustard.

BRIE IN A CRUST

*This is an easy before-dinner treat—the finished product is pleasing to the eye as well as the palate. The Brie is delicious when served with a **light** white wine. The delicate crust holds a delectable surprise. ENJOY!*

1 3-oz. package of
  cream cheese (room
  temperature)
½ cube (¼ cup) butter
  (room temperature)
¾ cup all purpose flour
1 miniature round Brie
  cheese (3 to 4½ oz.
  package)

In a medium size bowl cut the cream cheese and butter into flour with a pastry blender (I use a fork) until mixture resembles small peas. Shape into a ball, wrap in plastic wrap, refrigerate at least an hour. Divide the dough into 2 pieces. Roll out each piece to a 1/8th inch thickness (do this on a lightly floured surface). Cut each piece into a 6 inch circle, saving the excess for trim. On an ungreased cookie sheet, place one of the circles of dough, placing the round of cheese on top of circle. Top this with the other pastry circle and seal together as you do for a two-crusted pie. (I *flute* the edges and then I brush a little water on the edges of the crusts to help them seal). Roll out any excess dough and cut into designs. Place cut-outs on top of the crust. (I brush an egg wash on the dough to give it a nice finished look. (1 egg slightly beaten).

BAKE in a preheated 450 degree oven for 15 minutes until a light brown. Remove from oven and let stand about 5 minutes before cutting into small pie-shaped wedges. Best served warm. This should make about 12 small appeteaser wedges.

BONUS: Sprinkle sesame seeds on after the egg wash has been applied. This can be made the night before and

baked just before you serve it. Wrap
the Brie in Crust securely with plastic
wrap when holding overnight.

ASPARAGUS-BACON ROLLUPS

An elegant-looking appeteaser, tasty and easy to make.

12 slices white *sandwich*
  bread
1 container *whipped*
  cream cheese
12 fresh asparagus spears
  (or canned asparagus
  spears)
Crumbled bacon bits
  (West Virginia Brand is an
  excellent canned version)
Melted butter
Parmesan cheese

Cook the asparagus spears, drain and
cool.
Use a rolling pin to flatten out the
bread—cut off the crusts after you have
rolled over the bread—this gives an *up-town* finish to the rollups. Spread the
cream cheese over the bread slices,
sprinkle bacon bits over this, add the
asparagus spear and roll as for a
jellyroll. Cut each slice in half, place
on cookie sheet, brush each roll with
butter and sprinkle the Parmesan
cheese on top.

Bake in hot oven—400 degrees—until
the Parmesan has a golden glow. This
should take about 5—8 minutes but
watch closely so the rolls do not get
overglowed. You could also broil 6 inches from broiler until lightly toasted.

Yield: 24 appeteasers.

BONUS: These rolls can be made up
early in the day and refrigerated until
ready to pop in the oven. I have on occasion made them the night before I
baked them.

HAM & CHUTNEY TURNOVERS

A delightful light crust encases a flavorful ham and chutney combination. These mini-turnovers are a cinch to create.

1 cup butter
½ pound cream cheese
2 cups flour
2 cups chopped cooked ham
¾ cup chutney
2 or 3 dashes Tabasco

Make cream cheese pastry by working the butter and cream cheese into the flour (as you would make pie crust). Chill and roll out dough very thin (on a lightly floured bread board)—then cut out 3 inch rounds.

Plop rounded teaspoon of ham mixture on one side of the pastry round, fold over and crimp edges with a fork.

Bake on cookie sheet at 400 degrees— about 10 minutes or until lightly browned. Serve warm or room temperature.

BONUS: These yummy appeteasers can be frozen and reheated.

TEXAS CAVIAR

2 medium size cans of
blackeyed peas
1 cup salad oil
¼ cup wine vinegar
½ teaspoon salt
Ground pepper to taste
(I use about ¼ teaspoon)
1 clove garlic crushed
(or garlic salt to taste)
¼ cup dried minced onion

Drain the peas, add all remaining ingredients. Refrigerate for a week before enjoying. This is fun to serve with sesame seed crackers or any favorite cracker you might have hanging around the house. Just scoop up with a teeny spoon and plop on the cracker *you all.*

HONEY, BABE

*A cold-weather treat—the best version of a **hot whiskey** I've experienced.*

4 ounces whiskey
1½ cups boiling water
4 teaspoons honey
2 tablespoons whipped
  cream
Ground nutmeg

Dissolve the honey in boiling water. Add whiskey and shake it hard in a shaker if you have one gathering dust somewhere—if no dusty shaker—blend very well. Pour into tempered wine glasses or glass cups. Top with a *plop* of whipped cream and *freshly* ground nutmeg. YUM!

Yield: 2 cups

CAPPUCCINO

A scrumptious after-dinner coffee. Serve with Godiva chocolates if you are lucky enough to have some laying around the house...

1 cup of milk
3 heaping teaspoons
   chocolate milk mix
3 cups double strength coffee
   (or espresso—which is the
   ultimate)
¼ cup brandy
1 teaspoon vanilla
1 cup whipped cream

Heat the milk—stir in the chocolate milk mix
Add the 3 cups of coffee
Add vanilla and brandy
Add ¾ cup of the whipped cream

Gently stir all ingredients

Pour into cups and add the remaining whipped cream as garnish.

Yield: 8 half-cup servings

COFFEE MOCHA NUDGE

*This is a most lucious coffee dessert—easy to prepare and replaces the **usual** pie and cake routine.*

½ cup strong coffee
½ ounce Kahlua
½ ounce brandy
1 scoop coffee ice cream
Whipped cream for garnish
Chocolate curls or
   candied-coffee bean

In a clear, tempered coffee cup (or any other *tall* coffee mug, cup, etc.) pour in ½ cup of hot coffee, add the Kahlua and brandy (or a combination of Bailey's Irish Cream and Creme de Cacao or any other combination you like), plop in a scoop of ice cream, add a dollop of whipped cream, and top with a candied coffee bean or chocolate curls— serve with a spoon— and listen to the *m-m-m-yum's* abound. It is delicious. . .

HOT MULLED CIDER

Especially good when the leaves start to drop and Fall is in the air...

½ **cup brown sugar**
½ **teaspoon salt**
2 **quarts cider**
  (or apple juice)
1 **teaspoon whole allspice**
1 **teaspoon whole cloves**
3 **sticks of whole cinnamon**
Dash of fresh grated nutmeg

Combine brown sugar, salt and cider. Tie the spices in a small square of cheesecloth and add to cider mixture. Slowly bring to boil, cover and simmer 20 minutes. Remove the cheesecloth with spices. Serve hot in mugs.

Yield: 16 half cup servings or 8 mugs brim full.

ENGLISH TOFFEE FREEZ

*This smooth, refreshing **Freez** is a satisfying end to any day or night!*

4 **scoops English Toffee**
  ice cream
4 **ounces brandy**
4 **ounces half-and-half milk**
2 **ounces Creme de Cacao**
4 **ounces sweet chocolate bar**

Blend together the ice cream, brandy, half-and-half, and Creme de Cacao. Pour into stemmed glasses. Grate chocolate bar and sprinkle over top of Freez. Serve with straw and/or spoon.

Yield: 4 servings

SLUSHY DAIQUIRIS

An easy way to make a large batch of frozen daiquiris!

2 **large cans of frozen**
  lemonade
2 **large cans of frozen**
  limeade
1 **quart light Rum**
8 **cups water**

Mix all of the above ingreidents and store in the freezer. Remove from freezer, let mixture turn slushy and spoon into glasses.

MARGARITAS

Dig out that cocktail shaker and have a fling at making a stupendous Margarita to go along with your favorite Mexican entree.

Rub the rind of a fresh lime around rim of a 10-ounce cocktail glass—then dip the rim into a plate of coarse salt.

Pack the glass with crushed ice. Into a shaker full of ice, squeeze juice of half a lime. Use your fingers to give it a good squeeze— this will get some of the oil from the skin of the lime into the Margarita.

Add one-half ounce of good triple sec and 1½ ounces of good tequila. Shake it until thoroughly chilled—strain into the salted glass. OLE!

BRANDY SLUSH

*A refreshing, hot-weather slush—invite the gang over for **Brandy Snow Cones**...*

9 cups water
2 cups brandy
1—12 ounce can frozen
lemonade—thawed
1—12 ounce can frozen
orange juice, thawed
Fresh mint sprigs for garnish

Combine all ingredients except the mint in a four-quart container. Cover and freeze overnight. Mixture will remain slushy.
Spoon into individual glasses, garnish with mint (and spoon for those who cannot wait to test the savory results).

Yield: 3½ quarts

BANANA ZINGER

A great finale to a sumptious dinner.

1 very ripe banana
½ cup banana liqueur
¼ cup white Creme de Cacao
½ cup Half & Half cream
2 scoops banana ice cream
  (vanilla will do)
3 ice cubes
Nutmeg for garnish

Using a blender add all ingredients and blend away.

Yield: Four after-dinner goblet servings.

STRAWBERRY BLUSH

A good summertime punch—pretty and refreshing.

1 12-oz. can frozen lemonade
1 6-oz. can frozen limeade
1-2 pints strawberries—fresh
  or frozen—if fresh, slice
6 cups water
2 cups Vodka

1½ cups sugar
1 cup boiling water

7 Up

DISSOLVE 1½ cups sugar in 1 cup boiling water. Mix all other ingredients. Freeze.

Scoop slush into glasses, or glass cups, add 7-Up and serve.

SPIKED SANGRIA

10 bottles Red Table Wine
6 bottles carbonated water
(add just before serving)
1 small can frozen lemon
   juice
8 oz. Real Lemon juice
2 cups sugar
4 lemons (sliced thinly)
4 oranges (sliced thinly)

Make this 24 hours ahead—makes enough to serve 36 people.

RAMOS FIZZ

A very favorite of mine first experienced 20 years ago at the Edina Country Club in Minneapolis before a Green Bay Packer football game.

½ teaspoon sugar
Juice of ½ lemon
Juice of ½ lime
Dash of Orange Flower water
1 egg white
2 oz. heavy cream
2 oz. gin

Blend above with crushed ice Add Club soda and strain into champagne flutes.

BONUS: Depending on the size of the lemon and lime, and the amount of Club soda you use, you probably can get two servings from the above. When more servings are desired, I just double or triple the recipe or whatever—depends on the size of glasses you use. It's worth the extra effort.

GOLDEN FIZZ

Unlike the Ramos Fizz, I refer to this fizz as Golden because of the whole eggs used. The blender is a wonderful asset in concocting this fizz for a gaggle of guests in the early morning hours...their eyes will light up after the first sip!

6 whole eggs
1/2 can frozen lemonade
 concentrate, (thawed)
1 tablespoon powdered sugar
1/2 teaspoon vanilla extract
3/4 cup gin
3/4 cup whipping cream
Crushed ice

Combine the first four ingredients in a blender. Mix at medium speed until well blended. Add the gin, whipping cream and enough crushed ice to bring the level within 2 inches from the top of the blender. Turn on blender at lowest speed and continue by speeding up blender until all of the ice is pulverized.

Yield: 36 ounces = four—9 ounce servings or about eight—4 ounce servings—depending on what size wine glass you have in your cupboard.

BRANDY ALEXANDER

2 ounces Creme de cacao
2 ounces Brandy
3 scoops vanilla ice cream
1/2 cup half/half cream

Fresh grated nutmeg or
 chocolate curls

Put all ingredients in a blender (except garnish) and whirl away. Serve in a stemmed goblet as an after-dinner liquid dessert! Depending on size of glassware, you could serve four from the above concoction.

PEPPERMINT PATTY

2 ounces green Creme
de menthe
2 ounces white Creme
de cacao
3 scoops peppermint
ice cream
½ cup half/half

Crushed peppermint candy

Put all ingredients in a blender (except the garnish) and blend. Serve in after-dinner goblets and sprinkle some of the crushed peppermint candy on top—a great after-dinner dessert as is the Brandy Alexander—offer your guests a choice.

COFFEE NOG

A super nog. It is a tempting treat even for those calorie conscious persons. SERVE any time of the year—especially good during the holidays.

2 egg yolks
⅓ cup instant coffee
Pinch of salt
1 teaspoon vanilla
¼ cup sugar

Mix in blender

SLOWLY ADD:

3/4 cup brandy
2 cups milk

BLEND WELL—chill

JUST BEFORE SERVING ADD:

2 egg whites beaten
1 cup sugar
1 cup whipped cream

Makes about 8—10 cups

CHOCOLATE INSTANT NOG

1 quart dairy-case Egg Nog
3 ounces Hershey chocolate
   syrup
1/4 cup Creme de Cacao
1/4 cup brandy
2 heaping tablespoons
   instant Espresso coffee
   (powder form, not
   granuals)
1 cup whipping cream

Garnish:

Chocolate sprinkles, silver
   bead sprinkles, chocolate
   curls, or a chocolate candy
   coffee bean.

Combine the eggnog, chocolate syrup, Creme de Cacao, brandy and coffee powder—I use a wire whip—cover and chill.

Before serving fold half of the whipped cream into the eggnog mixture above, pour into serving glasses, put a *splotch* of whipped cream on top, and garnish.

BONUS: I make the eggnog mixture (without the whipped cream) the night before I use it so that the flavors have a chance to blend. Add the whipped cream before you serve it. If you have any left over, it can be refrigerated (I use an eggnog carton) and served later on. It will keep nicely for at least three of four days. This is a festive drink and used mostly during Thanksgiving and Christmas when the eggnog is available in the dairy case.

TOM & JERRY BATTER

*This comes from my family's **Scrapbook** of recipes. I remember my father making these in the **Mixmaster** for New Year's Eve...*

8 eggs—room temperature
½ teaspoon baking soda
2 pinches cream of tartar
1 teaspoon vanilla
1 teaspoon Rum

Separate yolks from whites

BEAT YOLKS 10 minutes or until light yellow in color and thick

BEAT WHITES 5 minutes until stiff but not dry.

FOLD yolks into whites adding carefully a one pound box of powdered sugar and the remaining ingredients.

TO SERVE:
Pour a small *jigger* of Rum and a small *jigger* of brandy in a heat-proof cup, add about a half cup of batter and fill the cup with hot water. A sprinkle of fresh-grated nutmeg is the finishing touch.

Yield: Depends on size and volume of eggs—I remember it made at least 12 generous servings.

BRUNCH:

BRUNCH:

Baked Potato Casserole - 52
Belgian Waffles - 42
Blina - 48
Crustless Crab Quiche - 46
Fluffy Egg Strata - 50
Gootch's Ebelskevers - 44
Ham 'N' Egg Scramble - 53
Hot Crab Souffle - 54
Link Sausage Brunch Casserole - 52
Old West Eggs and Cheese - 49
Oven Dutch Babies - 41
Scalloped Bacon & Eggs - 43
Stuffed Eggs Mornay - 47
Swiss Cheese Egg Bake - 51
Waffles LaRue - 42
Wild Rice and Sausage Delight - 45

OVEN DUTCH BABIES

YES, LORA & DAN—DUTCH BABIES ARE FOR REAL—ENJOY!

Pan size:	Butter:	Eggs:	Milk & Flour:
2-3 qts.	¼ cup	3	¾ cup each
3-4 qts.	⅓ cup	4	1 cup each

Select one of the above proportions to fit your ovenproof container (I use an oval 3 quart Pyrex *chicken* roaster—does that date me or does that date me???? You can use a *paella pan*, or large round quiche dish. You will want a shallow rimmed pan—about 3 inches—so that the batter *builds up.*

Put butter in the pan and set in 425 degree oven. Mix batter quickly as the butter melts. Put eggs in the blender and blend at high speed for 1 minute. While motor is running, gradually pour in milk, then slowly add the flour; continue blending for about 30 seconds. Add a teaspoon of vanilla for flavor. (If you do not have a blender, use a rotary-type eggbeater and beat the eggs until light and lemony colored, beat in the milk and then the flour).

Remove container from oven and pour batter into the hot melted butter. Return to oven and bake until *puffed* - 20 minutes or until light golden brown. Dust with powdered sugar and freshly ground nutmeg if you wish (by now, you have realized that I am *addicted* to fresh nutmeg—it is truly a tasty addition.) Slice in serving pieces and use syrup, fresh fruit—sweetened to taste; canned apple pie filling; or try: 1 box of frozen strawberries, add ½ cup sugar, heat until sugar dissolves—scrumptious.

3 quart size serves four people

BONUS: If you have a glass door on your oven—watch the progress of the Dutch Baby—it *builds up* into a mountainous shape. If you can't watch the progress, be sure your guests see it as it comes out of the oven as it will *fall* as it cools and they will miss the creation of the *Dutch Baby.*

WAFFLES LARUE

Feather light are these fantastic whipped cream waffles. Delicious any time of the day or night!

2 cups whipping cream
(old-fashioned not ultra-
pasteurized)
3 eggs, separated
1½ cups cake flour
1 level tablespoon sugar
¼ teaspoon salt
3 teaspoons baking powder
1 cup milk
2 tablespoons melted butter

Drop the egg yolks into the stiffly whipped cream one at a time, stirring until mixed. Sift the baking powder, flour, sugar and salt. Add the dry ingredients and milk alternately while mixing. Add the melted butter and then fold in the egg whites which have been stiffly beaten.
Bake in waffle iron.

BONUS: This makes a considerable batch of waffles because they are so light. They cook quickly and will be crisp. If you do not use all of the batter, it will keep up to a week in the refrigerator. Lightly whisk before using.

Follow the sequence of preparation for best results.

BELGIAN WAFFLES

*A most delectable attraction in Belgium—you can bake these in a standard electric waffle iron but in order to produce the authentic, Belgian waffles with their deep **crevices** to fill with warm maple syrup, fresh sliced strawberries and whipped cream, a special Belgian waffler is available in most gourmet cookware shops and in some department stores. Definitely a gastronomical delight.*

1 package dry yeast
2 cups lukewarm milk
4 eggs, separated
1 teaspoon vanilla

Heat milk to lukewarm, sprinkle yeast over the milk and stir to dissolve. Beat egg yolks and add to the yeast mixture, add vanilla.

2½ cups flour
½ teaspoon salt
1 tablespoon sugar
½ cup melted butter

Mix together the flour, salt and sugar—add to the liquid ingredients. Stir in the melted butter and combine thoroughly. Beat egg whites until stiff—carefully fold into the batter. At this point let the mixture stand in a warm place about 30 to 45 minutes or until mixture doubles in bulk. Pour a cup of mix into waffle iron and wait for light on the waffler to indicate that the waffle is done.

Yield: 5 Belgian waffles

BONUS: Should you by chance have a waffle or two left over, they will freeze and reheat in the oven very well. I wrap them separately in plastic wrap then in foil. Heat in a 375 degree oven for about 20 minutes. Take off plastic wrap but cover the waffles in foil before heating in the oven. They are as delicious as freshly made.

SCALLOPED BACON & EGGS

A slight variation of the Old West Eggs and Cheese.

¼ cup chopped onion
3 tablespoons flour
2 tablespoons butter
1½ cups milk
1 cup shredded Swiss
  cheese
½ teaspoon dry mustard
6 hard-boiled eggs sliced
1½ cups crunched potato
  chips
10 slices of bacon, fried crisp
  and crumbled

Saute onion in butter until transparent—do not brown. Stir in the flour—gradually add the milk, stirring constantly until thickened. Add the cheese and dry mustard—stirring until cheese is melted.

Divide the egg slices evenly in a buttered 10 x 6 inch baking dish—sprinkle with the salt and pepper. Cover with half each of the cheese sauce, crunched potato chips and crumbled bacon—repeat layers. Bake in preheated 350 degree oven—15—20 minutes.

GOOTCH'S EBELSKEVERS
(Danish Pancakes)

A tradition at Gootch's Sunday breakfast table. You must have an Ebelskever pan to achieve these tasty round, puffed pancakes. They are available in most kitchen gourmet shops and I have seen them in some department stores.

TOPPING:

1 cup sugar
1 package frozen
  strawberries

BATTER:

2 cups buttermilk
2 cups flour
3 eggs (separated)
1 teaspoon baking powder
1 teaspoon baking soda
2 tablespoons sugar
3 egg whites

¼ cup butter
¼ cup solid shortening

Put the strawberries and the cup of sugar in a medium saucepan and heat until boiling—turn down to simmer and cook until syrupy—about 10 minutes. Keep warm.

BATTER:

Mix flour, buttermilk, egg yolks, baking powder, baking soda and sugar with mixer until smooth. Beat egg whites separately until stiff but moist. Fold the whites gently by hand into the batter—taking care not to overmix—some large egg white lumps should *float* about.

MELT ¼ cup butter and ¼ cup solid shortening together in a cup with a pouring spout. Pour a little into each ebelskever *cup* each time you pour batter in.

HEAT the ebelskever pan over medium heat, then add a bit of melted butter and shortening in each cup; fill each cup about ⅔ full with the batter. After about 30 seconds little bubbles should appear like on pancakes—using a *pickle fork* or other metal skewer, turn the ebelskever over. Cook another 30 seconds to a minute. If no batter spurts through the shell—they are done. Sprinkle with powdered sugar, place in a heatproof serving bowl and keep warm in the oven until all of the batter has been used.

BONUS: This recipe will make about 35 ebelskevers—it depends on how big the cups are on ebelskever pan. However, I halve the batter portion of the recipe except for the eggs (I use two) and the batter will make about 21 ebelskevers.

All you need to serve with these tender round pancakes is crisp-broiled bacon, Canadian bacon or little link sausages.

WILD RICE AND SAUSAGE DELIGHT

Splurge and serve this flavorful hot dish for your next brunch. There is just nothing better than a dish made with wild rice.

1 cup wild rice
1 pound bulk sausage meat
6 ounce can of sliced
   mushrooms—improvise
   with fresh—they are great!
1 can condensed mushroom
   soup
1 medium white onion

Cook the rice el dente—not mushy. Drain. Brown the sausage (until crumbly).
Pour off fat, stir in the drained mushrooms and soup. Add to the wild rice. Put a layer of the rice mixture in a buttered casserole. Top with the onion which has been thinly sliced. Put another layer of the wild rice mixture over the top. Cover the casserole. Bake in 350 degree oven for 1 hour.

Yield: 6 side dish servings—can be doubled to serve more

BONUS: Make a day ahead or can be frozen.

CRUSTLESS CRAB QUICHE

This is a marvelous **crustless** *quiche—for those of you who do not want to tackle a pie crust—this is for you—no one will miss the crust...*

1 7½ ounce can of crabmeat
(Don't be a spendthrift on this—buy a good brand and get the *white lump* if you can)
1/2 pound fresh mushrooms, sliced
2 tablespoons butter
4 eggs
1 cup sour cream
1 cup small curd cottage cheese
1 cup fresh grated Parmesan cheese
¼ cup flour
1 teaspoon onion flakes (optional)
¼ teaspoon salt
6 drops Tabasco
2 cups shredded Monterey Jack cheese

Saute the mushrooms in the butter until tender. Remove mushrooms from the pan and drain on paper toweling. In a blender mix the eggs, sour cream, cottage cheese, Parmesan cheese, flour, onion flakes, salt and Tabasco.

Fold in the mushrooms, cheese and crabmeat. Pour into a 10 inch quiche dish. Bake at 350 degrees for 35 to 40 minutes or until golden and a knife inserted in center comes out the same way it went in—clean.

Let stand five minutes, cut and serve in wedges. Serves 8—10

BONUS: I cut the recipe in half except for the crabmeat and use a 9 inch pie pan—this still makes a very generous quiche and will serve 4 people with hearty appetites. This could also be a pleasant luncheon entree served with muffins, and a tart fruit or jello salad.

STUFFED EGGS MORNAY

*A perfect treat for a **Neighborhood Brunch**... as experienced by our Friendly Easter Brunch Bunch—Easter 1986. The high-schoolers, college crowd and **mature** group devoured the eggs in record time.*

10 tablespoons butter, melted
1 teaspoon salt
½ cup flour
Pinch of cayenne pepper
¼ teaspoon pepper
3 cups hot milk
½ cup shredded Swiss
   cheese
6 tablespoons grated
   Parmesan cheese (to be
   divided)
12 hard-boiled eggs
½ pound fresh mushrooms,
   finely chopped
2 tablespoons chopped
   parsley
½ teaspoon dried tarragon
1 cup fresh bread crumbs

Make a roux of 4 tablespoons butter, salt, flour, cayenne and pepper. Add milk and stir constantly over medium heat until sauce thickens. Add Swiss cheese and 4 tablespoons of the Parmesan. Stir until cheese melts. Set aside.

Cut the hard-boiled eggs in half; remove and mash yolks. Reserve the whites.

Saute mushrooms in 4 tablespoons of the butter until mixture until almost dry. Stir in parsley and tarragon. Add mushroom mixture to mashed egg yolks and stir in ½ cup of cheese sauce. Fill egg white halves with this mixture. Spread small layer of cheese sauce in shallow baking dish. Arrange stuffed egg halves in bottom and spoon remaining sauce over tops.

Toss bread crumbs with remaining 2 tablespoons melted butter and 2 tablespoons Parmesan cheese. Sprinkle over top of casserole.

Bake at 350 degrees for 30 minutes.

Yield: 12 servings—2 eggs each

BONUS: This recipe can be made ahead and refrigerated.

B L I N A
(Rolled German Pancake)

*A delightful German pancake which is very similar to a sour dough pancake-crepe combination. The **sponge** must be made the night before you prepare the blinas for consumption. Every German household has its favorite recipe, but basically—the pancakes taste the same. They are a very thin cake and easiest to cook in a crepe pan. A hot griddle will, however, suffice.*

1 package dry yeast
1 tablespoon sugar
3 cups all-purpose flour
3 cups warm water

²/₃ cup milk (scald and
  cool slightly)
½ teaspoon soda
1 tablespoon sugar
1 teaspoon salt

Dissolve the yeast and sugar in the warm water using a large bowl. Add the flour and beat until well mixed. Cover and keep unrefrigerated overnight. This sponge should rise during the night.

To the cooled milk, add 1 tablespoon sugar, the salt and soda. Stir well; add to the sponge.

Beat the three eggs and add to sponge, mixing well.

Pour ½ cup batter in greased 10 inch pan. Tilt to spread batter, brown, and turn over to brown the other side. Remove from pan, (at this point, I sprinkle a little powdered sugar on the blina and put in the oven to keep warm while I finish making the remainder of the pancakes). Let everyone prepare their blina by spreading with butter, syrup, honey, a yummy strawberry or huckleberry jam, or any other condiment, roll up jelly-roll fashion and enjoy. The pancakes should be crepe-like thin.

BONUS: Batter keeps well when covered in refrigerator. You can use the next day.

MY DAD SAYS *HEAT THE PLATES IN THE OVEN SO THE BLINAS WILL BE WARM WHEN YOU EAT THEM!*

OLD WEST EGGS AND CHEESE

The following Egg Dish is, I believe, actually called **continental** *- but I personally get tired of that much overused word so I have renamed it . . what's in a* **name** *any way?*

1 cup sliced white onion
1 tablespoon butter
8 hard-boiled eggs, sliced
2 cups shredded Swiss
  cheese (8 ounces)
1 can cream of chicken
  soup
¾ cup milk
1 teaspoon prepared mustard
½ teaspoon seasoned salt
  (such as Morton's
  seasoned salt)
¼ teaspoon dill weed
¼ teaspoon pepper
  (if you have a pepper mill,
  fresh ground gives an
  Old West PIZZAZ to the
  eggs)
6 slices Caraway Rye Bread—
  buttered and then cut
  into quarters

Preheat oven to 350 Degrees

Cook the onion in butter until just tender. Spoon this into a 12 x 8 inch baking dish. Divide the egg slices evenly over this, sprinkle with the cheese.

Beat remaining ingredients—except the bread, of course—in a bowl using a rotary hand beater. Pour this mixture over the cheese. At this point you can refrigerate—don't include the bread slices.

If you do not save overnight—then add the bread slices by overlapping them on top of the casserole and bake 30 to 35 minutes uncovered until heated through. If you do refrigerate overnight, add the bread slices just before baking and bake 40 to 45 minutes.

Yield: 8

FLUFFY EGG STRATA

*Aptly named because of its **add to** as the recipe progresses. Strictly an egg—cheese—no-meat dish and as close to being a soufflé as one can get. Brandied peaches and country-style sausages would be great with the Egg Strata.*

12 eggs—beat with mixer or rotary beater

Add:
½ cup all-purpose flour
1 teaspoon baking powder
½ teaspoon seasoned salt

Add:
(Fold in by hand all of the following *add to's*)
1 cup small curd cottage cheese
2 cups shredded Jack cheese
½ cup melted butter

Add:
1 tablespoon chives (fresh or dehydrated)
¼ teaspoon dry mustard
¼ teaspoon fresh ground pepper

Add:
1 can of chopped, seeded green chilies (an option but really tasty if included)

Pour into a buttered 9 x 13 inch baking pan and bake at 350 degrees for 35 minutes.

Yield: 12 servings

BONUS: Dabble 1 cup of alfalfa or radish sprouts over top of the Strata before serving. Also—a side dish of 1 can condensed cheddar cheese soup mixed with ¼ cup dry white wine and several splashes of Worcestershire is DELIGHTFUL!

SWISS CHEESE EGG BAKE

A nice egg side dish to serve with fresh fruit, cinnamon rolls, ham and lots of fresh-brewed coffee.

2 cans cream of chicken soup
1 cup milk
4 teaspoons minced onion
(dehydrated are
permissible)
1 teaspoon prepared mustard
2 cups grated Swiss cheese

Combine all ingredients except cheese. Heat on medium until warm and add the cheese.

Stir cheese until melted into the soup and milk mixture.

Pour 1 cup of the sauce into each of two 10 x 6 pans. Break six eggs into the sauce (three in-a-row down the length of the pan on each side). Carefully cover all BUT the yolks with the sauce.

Along the four edges of the pan line with slices of buttered french bread which have been *halved.*

Repeat the above procedure in the other pan.

BAKE for 20 minutes at 350 degrees or until the eggs are done to your desire—the eggs will *cover* themselves as they bake.

BONUS: If you use this dish for *youngsters* and adults—you will be surprised how many the *youngsters* will inhale.

BAKED POTATO CASSEROLE

*If you want to treat your family and friends to something special and can do it in **one fell swoop** - try this prepare-ahead meat and potato entree.*

2 pounds potatoes
(depending on size—about
6 bakers)
2 cups cubed ham
5 eggs
1 cup milk
½ teaspoon salt
¼ teaspoon dill weed
½ teaspoon marjoram
¼ teaspoon pepper
1 cup shredded cheddar
cheese

Cook the potatoes in their jackets until *fork-tender.* Cool, peel and slice into ½ inch slices. In a buttered 12 x 8 inch baking dish, alternate the sliced potatoes and the ham. Arrange the cheese over this.

Combine the rest of the ingredients and pour over top of the potatoes and ham. At this point you can refrigerate until the next morning.

Bake uncovered at 375 degrees for 30 to 35 minutes or until a knife inserted near middle of the casserole comes out clean (as you would test for a custard, quiche, etc.). Garnish with fresh parsley if you have some in the house or garden.

Yield: Should serve 8—10 nicely— depends on whether your friends are good eaters or *dieters.*

LINK SAUSAGE
BRUNCH CASSEROLE

1½ pounds link sausage
8 slices bread, trimmed
and cubed
2 cups grated sharp cheddar
cheese

Butter a 2 quart casserole. Cut the sausages in half and brown. Arrange the bread cubes in the casserole pan. Top with the browned sausage and cover with the cheese.

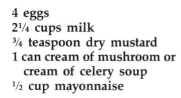

4 eggs
2¼ cups milk
¾ teaspoon dry mustard
1 can cream of mushroom or
   cream of celery soup
½ cup mayonnaise

Beat the eggs with the milk and dry mustard—pour this over the bread cubes and refrigerate overnight.

Next day—mix together the can of soup, ½ cup mayonnaise and pour over top of the casserole. Bake for 1 hour at 325 degrees.

Yield: 8—10 servings.

BONUS: I like Orange Bow Knots and a tart fruit mixture with this sausage dish.

HAM 'N' EGG SCRAMBLE

A very tasty method of serving Ham and Eggs for breakfast and without all the mess—just prepare it the night before and have it ready to pop into the oven for an early breakfast or later brunch!

1 cup diced ham
4 green onions with some
   of the tops—thinly sliced
4 tablespoons margarine or
   butter
1 dozen eggs—beaten
½ cup fresh mushrooms—
   sliced
1 recipe Cheese Sauce
   (to follow)
2 tablespoons butter melted
2 cups fresh (soft) bread
   crumbs (about 4 slices
   bread)

CHEESE SAUCE: Melt 2 tablespoons butter, blend in 2 tablespoons all-purpose flour, ½ teaspoon salt, dash

In large skillet, cook the ham and onion in the 4 tablespoons butter or margarine until onion is tender—do not brown. Add the beaten eggs and mushrooms—scramble just until eggs are *softly* cooked.

FOLD the egg mixture into the Cheese sauce and pour into a 12 x 7 baking dish. Combine the remaining 2 tablespoons of butter or margarine with the bread crumbs (easiest to get the bread *crumby* - use food processor or blender) and sprinkle on top of the casserole.

Cover and chill the egg mixture until ½ hour before baking in a 350 degree oven for ½ hour.

of pepper, add 2 cups of milk (as for making a white sauce). Cook over medium heat until thickened—Stir in 1 cup shredded mild cheddar cheese or process American cheese until melted.

Yield: 10—12 servings

BONUS: You can prepare this dish the night before you plan to use it. Just refrigerate overnight and bake the next morning.

HOT CRAB SOUFFLÉ

A very tasty and impressive soufflé—simple to assemble the night before that Sunday brunch you have been putting off. TRY IT SOON!

8 slices white bread
2 cups crab (or 2 cans)
½ cup mayonnaise
1 onion, finely chopped
1 green pepper, finely chopped
1 cup of finely, chopped celery
4 eggs
3 cups milk
1 can cream of celery soup
1 cup grated sharp cheddar cheese
Paprika

Trim crusts from bread, cube 4 slices of the bread and scatter into a buttered 2 quart casserole (you can use a round pottery casserole dish or a "flat Pyrex" dish).

MIX the crab, mayonnaise, onion, green pepper and celery, spread on the diced bread.

Place the remaining four slices of trimmed and cubed bread over the crab mixture. Pour eggs and milk mixture over the above.

Refrigerate overnight. Next day remove from refrigerator, bake at 325 degrees for 15 minutes, take out of oven and spoon the soup over the top, sprinkle the cheese over soup and shake a little paprika on top of cheese (the paprika is optional). Bake for 1 hour longer.

Yield: This serves 12 people adequately.

BONUS: Marinated Mushroom/ Artichoke Salad is good with this soufflé.

BREADS:

BREADS:

MILLIE'S SWEET ROLL DOUGH

2 packages dry yeast
½ cup warm water
2½ cups milk
¼ cup (1 cube) margarine
⅔ cup sugar
2 teaspoons salt
4 eggs
8½ to 9 cups flour

Dissolve the 2 packages of yeast in the warm water.

Combine the milk, margarine, sugar and salt in a medium sauce pan and heat just until margarine is melted. Remove from heat.

In large mixing bowl—beat the eggs (with a fork until completely mixed), add the yeast mixture to the eggs and then add the milk mixture which has cooled somewhat.
Add the flour gradually so that it becomes a soft dough. If you have a mixer with a dough hook you can utilize it here. If you have to beat the flour in by hand (as I do) use a long handled wooden spoon— I found that this works the best—or if you have a strong-armed friend at hand—drag him or her into the kitchen and promise a nice hot cinnamon roll for their *heroics*.

The dough will be soft. Do not knead. Let rise—until double in size. Punch down and proceed with any kind of sweet rolls. I like to use the dough for cinnamon rolls or butter pecan rolls.

Yield: Depends on what kind of rolls you make. I get about three dozen cinnamon or butter pecan rolls.

BUTTER PECAN ROLLS

*Use **Millie's Sweet Roll Dough** in perfecting these scrumptious caramelized Butter Pecan Rolls. This version is the best sticky-bun caramel roll that I could muster out of many experiments. I hope you will approve my efforts.*

3 tablespoons butter, melted
¼ cup granulated sugar
1 teaspoon ground cinnamon
⅓ cup packed brown sugar
¼ cup butter (do not
   use margarine)
1 tablespoons light
   corn syrup
¼ cup chopped pecans

Roll out one-third of Millie's Sweet Roll Dough into a 12x8-inch rectangle. Brush with the 3 tablespoons of melted butter. Combine granulated sugar and cinnamon; sprinkle over the dough. Roll up the dough, starting with long side; seal seam. Slice roll into 12 pieces.

In saucepan, combine the brown sugar, ¼ cup butter and corn syrup. Cook and stir just until butter melts and mixture is blended. Distribute the mixture evenly in baking pan. Top with pecans. Place rolls, cut side down, in prepared baking pan. Cover; let rise until double (about 30 minutes).

Bake at 375 degrees for 18 to 20 minutes. Cool about 30 seconds; invert on a sheet of foil.

Yield: 12

BONUS: Triple the ingredients if you plan to use the full recipe of Millie's Sweet Roll Dough and strew evenly on three rectangles of dough.

CINNAMON ROLLS

*Use **Millie's Sweet Roll Dough** for these luscious cinnamon rolls. They are super served any time of the day OR night!*

2 tablespoons butter
²/₃ cup brown sugar
2 teaspoons ground
  cinnamon
½ cup chopped walnuts
  (optional)
½ cup currants or raisins

CONFECTIONER'S ICING:

Combine 1 cup sifted powdered sugar, ¼ teaspoon vanilla and enough milk to make a *drizzling* consistency - about 1½ tablespoons.

Roll out one-third of Millie's Sweet Roll Dough into 12x8-inch rectangle. Brush with the melted butter.

Combine the brown sugar, walnuts, currants OR raisins and ground cinnamon. Sprinkle atop the rectangle of dough. Roll up from long side; seal seams.

Slice into 12 rolls.

Place in greased baking pans, cover; let rise until double (about 30 minutes).
Bake at 375 degrees for 18 to 20 minutes—or until lightly browned on top. Cool slightly, and remove from pans at this point—or leave in pans if you want.
Drizzle with Confectioner's Icing

BONUS: I like to add a bit of fresh lemon juice to the Confectioner's Icing—if you choose to do so—use less milk.

SWEDISH COFFEE TWISTS

*Wonderful **Cinnamon-like soft breadsticks** are these ... Relatively easy to do, the twists are good served for breakfast, brunch, with soups, etc. You will want to keep some in the freezer.*

1 package active dry yeast
¼ cup warm water
1 cup buttermilk
6 tablespoons margarine
3 tablespoons sugar
1 teaspoon salt
1 egg, slightly beaten
¼ teaspoon baking soda

3—4 cups all-purpose flour

CINNAMON FILLING:
Mix:
¼ cup firmly packed brown
   sugar
½ teaspoon cinnamon.

SUGAR GLAZE:
Beat together:
1½ cups powdered sugar
1 tablespoon melted butter
   or margarine
2 tablespoons hot water.

Sprinkle yeast into water in a small bowl—stirring to blend. Over medium heat, bring the buttermilk just to boiling (it will separate). Put 4 tablespoons of the margarine, sugar and salt in large bowl and pour in the buttermilk. Stir to melt the margarine—cool to lukewarm. Blend in softened yeast and egg. Stir in soda, then gradually stir in the flour until a soft dough just cleans the sides of the bowl.

Turn onto a floured board and knead until smooth and elastic, adding up to ½ cup flour as needed to prevent sticking. Invert bowl over dough and let stand 15 minutes.

Punch down dough; roll out into a 12x20-inch rectangle. Melt the remaining 2 tablespoons margarine and brush it over the surface of the dough.

Sprinkle cinnamon filling lengthwise over one-half of the dough. Fold rectangle in half lengthwise to cover filling; press edges together. Cut dough crosswise in 26 strips so that each strip is ¾ inches wide. Twist each strip twice and place about 1 inch apart on greased baking sheets. Let rise uncovered in a warm place until puffy— about 45 minutes.

Bake in 375 degree oven for about 12 minutes or until pale golden. Remove to rack, let cool slightly and brush with Sugar Glaze.

BONUS: To reheat, place twists, uncovered in 375 degree oven for about 5 minutes.

AUNT LIZZIE'S ORANGE BOW KNOTS

Bountiful are recipes for Orange Rolls—but Aunt Lizzie's remain on top of the heap as far as my taste buds go. Their shape is also very appealing.

1¼ cups milk—scalded
1 cube margarine or shortening (½ cup)
⅓ cup sugar
1 teaspoon salt
1 package active dry yeast (original recipe calls for 1 yeast cake)
5 cups all-purpose flour
2 eggs—beaten
¼ cup fresh orange juice
2 tablespoons grated orange peel

GLAZE:
2 tablespoons orange juice
1 teaspoon grated orange peel
1 cup powdered sugar

Scald together the milk, margarine, sugar, salt—cool to lukewarm. Add the yeast to this mixture.

Add eggs, orange juice and peel. Beat well, add flour and mix to soft dough. Cover and let stand 10 minutes. Knead on a lightly floured board—about 8 minutes. Place in greased bowl, let rise in warm place until doubled in bulk—or about 2 hours. Punch down and divide dough into thirds. Roll each third into a one-half inch thick rectangle. Cut ten strips—each one-half inch wide—tie each in a Knot, place on greased baking sheet and let rise again until double.

Bake in 400 degree oven about 15 minutes or until light golden.

Place on rack and cool slightly—glaze.

Yield: 3 dozen

BONUS: Can be frozen and reheated.

COFFEE CINNAMON COFFEE CAKE

If you are addicted to coffee—you'll appreciate Coffee Cinnamon Coffee Cake—not only for the flavor, but the scent of this cake baking in the oven is more than you bargained for...

1 cube unsalted butter—
  softened
1 cup granulated sugar
2 eggs
1 tablespoon strong coffee
½ teaspoon vanilla
2 cups all-purpose flour
1 teaspoon baking powder
1 teaspoon baking soda
Pinch of salt
1¼ cups dairy sour cream
¼ cup currants
½ cup packed dark brown
  sugar
⅓ cup finely chopped
  pecans or walnuts
2 teaspoons cinnamon
2 teaspoons instant coffee
  powder (not granules)

GLAZE:
1 cup powdered sugar
2 tablespoons strong coffee
½ teaspoon milk
½ teaspoon vanilla

Cream the butter and sugar in large mixer bowl. Beat in the eggs one at a time—beating well; add 1 tablespoon strong coffee and the vanilla.

Blend together the flour, baking powder, baking soda and salt—add the flour mixture to the butter mixture—alternating with the sour cream. Hold aside.

Soak currants in hot water to cover 10 minutes; drain and combine with brown sugar, nuts, cinnamon and instant coffee powder, in a small bowl.

Butter a 12-cup Bundt pan or 10-inch tube pan. Spread one-fourth of the reserved batter into bottom, sprinkle with a third of currant mix. REPEAT layering twice—end with batter on top.

Bake at 375 degrees for 55 minutes—test for doneness with wooden pick inserted in center. Remove from oven and cool on wire rack.

SPOON GLAZE over cake after removing from pan.

BONUS: Instead of soaking the currants in hot water, add a gourmet's touch by soaking the currants in 3 tablespoons Cognac or Brandy before adding to the batter. This coffee cake freezes splendidly!

MARGE'S CARAMEL ROLLS

Most delightful and effortless—assemble the night before and surprise your family with a pan of these scrumptious caramel rolls for breakfast.

1 package commercially
  frozen dough for rolls
½ of a 3 1/8-ounce package
  dry butterscotch pudding
  mix (DO NOT USE
  INSTANT PUDDING
  MIX)
½ cup margarine
¾ cup brown sugar
¾ cup chopped pecans

Butter a Bundt pan, angel food pan or 2 loaf pans.

Sprinkle bottom of pan with the one-half package of butterscotch pudding mix.

Melt the margarine (reserve 2 tablespoons) with the brown sugar and pour evenly over top of the pudding mix—then divide the nuts over all.

Arrange the frozen rolls on top of the above mixture. Drizzle the reserved 2 tablespoons melted margarine over the rolls.

Cover the pan with foil and let rise 12 hours or overnight.

Next morning, pop the rolls into a 350 degree oven for 20 to 30 minutes. Remove from oven and immediately turn pan upside down on another piece of foil to cool.

POTICA BREAD
a/k/a NUT ROLLS

*A wondrous delight—not an easy task—but the end result is certainly worth the effort. Potica bread is usually reserved for Thanksgiving and Christmas festivities, but one does not have to **hold off** until then to create and ENJOY!*

**2 packages instant dry yeast
dissolved in ¼ cup
warm water
2 cups milk—scalded
2 teaspoons salt
¼ cup sugar
¼ cup butter
(don't substitute)
2 eggs well beaten
8 cups all-purpose flour**

NUT FILLING:

**1 cup half-and-half milk
1 pound walnuts,
ground fine
(use food processor
or blender)
3 eggs (unbeaten)
1 cup honey
½ cup sugar**

**Mix the above ingredients
well.**

Dissolve yeast in water. Scald the milk; combine hot milk, salt, sugar and butter. Blend thoroughly. Cool to lukewarm, add the eggs and yeast.

Put 6 cups of flour into a large bowl, gradually adding milk mixture. Beat until sticky dough is accomplished. Add remainder flour (2 cups) or enough to make a soft dough.
Place on well-floured board and knead at least 15 minutes (you may have to take a little R&R (rest and relaxation) during this activity...
Place in a large greased bowl, cover with a damp cloth, let rise in warm place until double in bulk (probably will take at least 2 hours).
Separate dough in half. Roll out half of the dough as for cinnamon rolls—except much, much thinner.
Spread with half of the nut filling, roll up jelly-roll style, sealing ends. Place on cookie sheet in S shape.
Bake for 20 minutes at 375 degrees then REDUCE HEAT to 325 degrees and continue baking for another 20 minutes.

Yield: Makes two large S shaped rolls.

BONUS: You can divide the original dough into fourths and make four smaller rolls. The rolls freeze well so

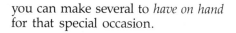

you can make several to *have on hand* for that special occasion.

CELERY ROLLS IN A LOAF

*This is not a loaf of bread that you have to create from **scratch**. Purchase a loaf of unsliced white bread from your local supermarket bakery and create an impressive accompaniment to an entree of your choice...Your guests will marvel at your culinary skills.*

1 small loaf unsliced
  white bread
½ cup softened butter
  (don't substitute)
1 teaspoon celery seed
¼ teaspoon salt
¼ teaspoon paprika
Generous dash of cayenne

Trim crusts from top, sides and ends of loaf. Cut down through center of loaf almost to bottom of crust—making about ½ inch slices as you go.

Mix together the softened butter, celery seed, salt, paprika and cayenne. Spread the mixture over the entire surface of cuts.

Place on baking sheet; cover with plastic wrap and refrigerate for at least an hour.

Bake in a 400 degree oven for 15 minutes or until golden.

Yield: As many slices as you make— at least 8 to 10.

BONUS: You could use a wheat bread if you prefer.

BJ'S ALPHA-DOUGH-ME'S
(Soft Breadsticks)

*Definitely a **Family Affair** - originated by my sister-in-law Bertie, perfected by me and christened **Alpha-Dough-Me's** by my husband. Alpha-Dough-Me's are soft breadsticks that can be fashioned into many shapes and sizes to fit any occasion. . there simply are no limitations. Alpha-Dough-Me's are exciting, fascinating and satiable.*

1 can—refrigerated commercial Soft Breadsticks
Coarse ground salt, sesame seeds, poppy seeds, caraway seeds, fresh grated orange rind, parmesan cheese, etc., etc.

Greased cookie sheets
Two healthy arms
Scads of imagination

Separate the breadsticks upon opening the can.

Standing near a table or countertop—with plenty of *air space* above you—hold one dough breadstick about an arm's length in front of you - one end in each hand held by thumbs and forefingers. Stretch the dough out and twirl the breadstick three or four times—as you would in jumping rope. Let it stretch out about twice the original length, let go of one end and standing over a cookie sheet, form an initial, number, heart, tree, etc., by writing it all in one-fell-swoop.

The quicker you move with the breadstick dough, the better so that it doesn't have a chance to *shorten up* to its original size. You can cut off a separate piece of the dough before starting your creation if you need an *add-on* such as for an F, T. H, etc.—depends on how you form it.

You may want to practice a couple of times, but don't be afraid to stretch the dough out and reuse it—as soon as you get the hang of it you can create to your heart's content! It is wonderful therapy.

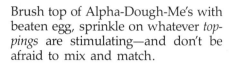

Brush top of Alpha-Dough-Me's with beaten egg, sprinkle on whatever *toppings* are stimulating—and don't be afraid to mix and match.

Bake in preheated 350 degree oven for 15—18 minutes or until golden. Remove and cool on racks.

BONUS: Best served day of creation but will freeze and reheat adequately. Let your imagination go crazy—there are multitudinous creative ideas just waiting to be captured. Try a powdered sugar lemon or fresh orange frosting glaze and brush on while Alpha-Dough-Me's are still warm— they are scrumptious with coffee, tea or milk. VOILA!!

DIXIE'S SKY HIGH BISCUITS

*If you have never tackled a **baking-powder biscuit** like the ones grandma used to make—try your luck with these—you'll be glad you did. They are surprisingly fluffy and **sky-high**.*

3 cups all-purpose flour
4½ teaspoons baking powder
2 tablespoons granulated sugar
½ teaspoon salt
¾ teaspoon cream of tartar

¾ cup butter or margarine

1 egg beaten
1 cup milk

Combine the first five ingredients. Cut in the butter or margarine until mixture is coarse and crumbly (resembles a pie crust dough—if you know what that is supposed to look like). Add the beaten egg and milk—stirring quickly and until just mixed. On a lightly floured bread board—knead briefly. Roll (or pat with heel of hands) to about a 1 inch thickness. Cut the biscuits with a round biscuit cutter. Place on cookie sheet.

Bake in preheated 425 degree oven for 12 to 15 minutes.

SCIOCCO

*Sciocco—pronounced **Scotch-oh** is a Sicilian bread familiarly Italian and redolent of cheeses, sausage and Italian spices. Sciocco takes some time and effort to create but it is worth every minute to get to the finished product. It can be served cold or warm—as a picnic entree, lunch at the ski hill or a Sunday night supper—a ¾ inch slice is perfect—no thicker or thinner. Those who are lucky enough to partake will praise your skillfulness...try it soon!*

1 package active dry yeast
1/8 teaspoon sugar
1¼ cups warm water
½ teaspoon salt
2½ to 3 cups all-purpose
   flour

1 onion, minced
   (approximately ⅔ cup)
3 tablespoons butter

1—15 ounce can tomato sauce
2 tablespoons heavy cream
¼ teaspoon dried oregano
   leaves
¼ teaspoon dried basil
   leaves
½ teaspoon salt
Freshly ground pepper
¾ cup chopped fresh
   parsley leaves (about
   one bunch)

1 pound mild Italian sausage
1½ teaspoons olive oil

2 tablespoons olive oil
½ cup Ricotta cheese
¾ cup shredded provolone
   cheese
Cornmeal

Dissolve yeast with sugar in ¼ cup of the water in a large bowl; let stand 10 minutes until bubbly. Stir in remaining water, the salt and 2 cups of flour—to make a sticky but workable dough; turn dough onto a floured surface and knead the remaining flour in until smooth and elastic—10 minutes. Place dough in greased bowl; turn greased side up and cover; let rise until double—at least 2 hours.

Saute onion in butter until transparent. Stir in tomato sauce, cream, oregano and basil; simmer—stirring occasionally over low heat. Cook sauce about 45 minutes. Season with salt and pepper, stir in parsley. Reserve.

Pierce the sausage with fork at 1—inch intervals. Brown in 1½ teaspoons olive oil over medium heat—10 minutes. Cook covered 5 minutes and cool slightly; cut into ¼ inch slices. Reserve.

Punch down dough; knead on lightly floured board for 4 minutes. Roll out on floured surface into a 16 x 12 inch rectangle and brush with 2 tablespoons of the olive oil. Spread tomato

Olive oil

sauce over dough as for pizza; arrange the sausage over tomato sauce and dot with ricotta; sprinkle with shredded cheese.

Beginning at the longer edge, fold over a 3-inch section of dough; fold over again. Tuck ends under and place the loaf seam-side down on a baking sheet sprinkled with cornmeal. Cover; let rise until double - about 1 hour.

Heat oven to 350 degrees. Brush the loaf with olive oil; pierce several times with fork and bake in upper part of oven about one hour or until loaf tests done (should sound hollow when tapped).

Serve in ¾ inch slices.

Yield: 10 to 12 servings

BONUS: This freezes very well—so you can make Sciocco and reserve a space in the freezer until a special outing looms on the horizon.

HUGH FORD'S POTATO ROLLS

*DO NOTHING OR LEAVE NOTHING IN DRAFT ... simply stated but forewarned. These words lead the recipe Hugh gave to me many years ago. These rolls were part of Hugh's mother's collection of recipes and he gave me the recipe as he **learned** the proper measurements.*

1 cup fresh mashed potatoes (1 large white or two small) cooked until mealy. Drain off excess water.

While boiling potatoes, mix one package of dry yeast with 1 cup tepid water.

Mash potatoes thoroughly and add ½ cup unmelted Crisco, ¼ cup sugar and 1 teaspoon salt—beat together. Then add 1 cup cold water and let set until tepid or cooler.

Add dissolved yeast and water. Mix thoroughly. Add 2 eggs beaten in ½ cup cold water. Stir up mixture. Then add 2 cups all-purpose flour. Mix. Let set in warm area..not hot..covered with a dry cloth until batter doubles and is bubbling.

Stir down, gradually add 4 more cups of flour, stirring in one at a time. Cover with dry cloth until double in size .. out of draft. When double, stir down and put in refrigerator covered with a damp cloth. Keep cloth damp. Leave in refrigerator at least overnight.

Stir down before using and then take out what dough you need and return the balance to refrigerator and cover with damp cloth again. Dough will keep in refrigerator one week. Stir down each time before using.

BAKING: Grease muffin tin generously with Crisco. After rolls are made up (use enough dough to half fill muffin cup)—let them double in size before baking. May take an hour or more, but the important thing is that they double — no matter what the time.

Brush rolls with melted butter before baking for better crust.

Bake approximately 25 minutes (Montana altitude) in preheated 350 degree oven.

Yield: 24 muffin-size rolls.

PEFFERNAISE DINNER ROLLS

*Peffernaise dinner rolls are **traditionally** German in origin. Many, many variations exist but basically contain the same ingredients, including black pepper and Anise. Try these for a change of pace at your next dinner party. The rolls are **heavier** than regular breads.*

1 package dry yeast
2 cups lukewarm water
½ cup sugar
6 cups flour
1 tablespoon salt
½ cup molasses
4 tablespoons melted
  shortening
1 egg—well beaten
1 cup pumpkin
1 teaspoon Anise powder
  or extract
Pinch of pepper

In large bowl add yeast to water and stir; add sugar, salt, molasses, pumpkin and egg. Add one-half of the flour (3 cups) and beat well. Stir in the melted shortening, pepper and/or Anise powder and remainder of the flour—mix well.

Knead on floured board at least 10 minutes—this is important step. Cover and let rise until double in bulk—about 1½ hours. Punch down and let rise until doubled (cover with damp cloth).

Shape into desired rolls, let rise in pan about 1 hour.

Bake at 350 degrees for 25—35 minutes.

Yield: Depends on what shape you use for rolls. (2—3 dozen)

KAY'S ONION BUNS

*Those of the populous who do not **do breads** are surely missing out—and particularly savory are these onion buns accompanying that first Spring or Summer outing—whether it be a backyard barbecue or camping **safari**.*

3 tablespoons butter or
  margarine
¾ cup finely chopped
  onions
3 cups all purpose flour
3 cups whole wheat flour
3 tablespoons sugar
1 teaspoon salt
2 packages active dry yeast
2 cups hot tap water

In a small fry pan, heat the butter, add onions and saute 5 minutes until golden. Set aside.

In a large mixer bowl—blend 1 cup all-purpose flour and 1 cup whole wheat flour, the sugar, salt and yeast. Reserve 2 tablespoons of the *butter-onion* mixture and blend remainder into the yeast mixture; pour in the hot tap water and beat on low speed for 2 minutes. Add 1 cup whole wheat flour and beat on high speed for 2 minutes. Stir in remaining 1 cup whole wheat flour and 1 cup white flour. Sprinkle ⅓ cup of the remaining regular white flour on bread board, turn out dough and knead until smooth and elastic (about 5 minutes). Add flour if needed. Place in greased bowl, grease top of dough and cover—let rise until double in size (about 1 hour).

Punch down, roll out (about 1 inch thickness) and cut in 4 inch rounds. Place on greased cookie sheet, spread with remaining onion butter. Cover and let rise until double—45—50 minutes.

Bake in preheated 375 degree oven for 20 to 25 minutes.

Yield: 20—22 rolls

BONUS: Can be made ahead of time and frozen. You can shape into hotdog buns also.

HONEY WHOLE WHEAT LOAF

Absolutely my favorite bread—it utilizes wheat and honey, two products that lend to healthy beings and is particularly good toasted.

2 packages active dry yeast
½ cup warm water
⅓ cup honey
¼ cup vegetable shortening (not oil)
1 tablespoon salt
1¾ cups warm water
3 cups whole wheat flour
3 to 4 cups all-purpose flour
Margarine or butter, softened

In a large mixing bowl, dissolve the yeast in the ½ cup warm water. Stir in honey, shortening, salt, 1¾ cups warm water and the whole wheat flour. Beat until smooth. Mix in enough all-purpose white flour to make the dough easy to handle. (Should not be sticky).

Turn dough out onto a lightly floured surface; knead until smooth and elastic—about 8 minutes. Place in a greased bowl—turning greased side up. Cover with a towel and let rise in a warm place until doubled—1 hour. (Dough is ready if indentation remains when touched).

Punch the dough down and divide in half. Flatten each half with rolling pin into rectangle, 18 x 9 inches. Beginning with the narrow end, roll dough up jelly roll style; seal edge and ends.

Place sealed side down in greased baking pans, 9x5x3. Brush with melted butter; sprinkle with whole wheat flour or oatmeal flakes or leave plain. Let rise about 1 hour—or until doubled.

Bake in a preheated 375 degree oven until loaves are deep golden and

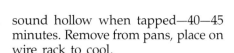

sound hollow when tapped—40—45 minutes. Remove from pans, place on wire rack to cool.

Yield: 2 loaves

BONUS: Eat one loaf and freeze the other. Of course, it is yummiest warm out of the oven with lots of butter and homemade huckleberry jam...just thinking about it activates the *drooling* process.

MORAVIAN LOVE BUNS

*Take whatever thoughts you desire from the title of this recipe. The Love Buns are sweeter and softer than an ordinary **dinner roll** and are definitely not run-of-the mill. Besides their tastiness—the buns offer up great comments at the dining table...*

1 **large potato**
1 **package dry yeast**
¼ **cup warm water**
½ **cup butter—melted**
1 **cup sugar**
1 **teaspoon salt**
2 **eggs, well beaten**
4 **cups sifted all purpose flour**

Pare the potato, cut in chunks and cook in boiling water until tender. Drain—save ½ cup of the potato water. Mash potato until smooth and measure out ½ cup.
Sprinkle yeast over the ¼ cup warm water to dissolve.
Combine mashed potato, ½ cup of the reserved potato water, butter, sugar, salt and eggs.
When mixture is lukewarm, stir in the yeast. Cover with a towel and set bowl in a warm place until dough becomes spongy-looking. Then mix in the flour thoroughly. (At this point the dough should be *soft* - if sticky—add a little more flour). Cover and let rise in a warm spot until double in size.
Punch down the dough and knead on a floured board until smooth (about 5 minutes).

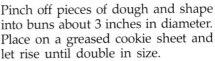

Pinch off pieces of dough and shape into buns about 3 inches in diameter. Place on a greased cookie sheet and let rise until double in size.
Bake in preheated 375 degree oven for 25—30 minutes.
When buns just begin to turn golden, brush the tops with a little cream or melted butter.
Cool before serving.

Yield: 1 dozen

BONUS: You can vary the size of the Love Buns—they make marvelous sandwich or hamburger buns.

JOHNNY CAKE

I'm not sure where to categorize Johnny Cake—it's not really a cake nor is it strictly a bread—it fits somewhere in between. It is similar to cornbread. Regardless of its **direction** *- it can be utilized for whatever you choose to serve with it.*

1¹⁄₃ **cups flour**
²⁄₃ **cup finely ground corn meal**
4 teaspoons baking powder
¹⁄₂ **teaspoon salt**
¹⁄₄ **cup melted butter— cooled a bit**
2 eggs
²⁄₃ **cup milk**
¹⁄₃ **cup Maple syrup**

Mix together the first four ingredients in large bowl.

Gradually stir in by hand last four ingredients.

Butter a 9x9-inch square baking pan and spoon batter into it.

Bake at 375 degrees for 25 minutes.

Yield: Serves 10

BONUS: Johnny Cake is good served warm with butter and Maple syrup— it can be served for breakfast or brunch together with some crispy bacon or sausages.

KRAUT BIEROCKS

Anyone from a German background should be familiar with these **German-style Pasties.** *My grandmother made them with cabbage and they were called* **Cabbage Bread.** *I do not like her version because they are very bland. The addition of kraut and sausage is both* **fragrant** *and delectable.*

½ cup vegetable shortening
  (Crisco)
¼ cup sugar
1 cup bran flakes
1 cup boiling water
1 package dry instant yeast
1 beaten egg
1 teaspoon salt
3 cups all-purpose flour
½ pound lean ground
  hamburger
½ cup country-style sausage
½ medium onion—chopped
1½ cups sauerkraut—drained
Salt and pepper to taste

Combine the shortening, sugar and bran flakes in large bowl; pour the boiling water over. Stir and cool. Add yeast, egg, salt and flour. Knead dough about 5 minutes. Place in greased bowl, greased side up, cover with towel and let rise—about 1 hour.

Meanwhile—cook hamburger and sausage until tender but not overly browned; add sauerkraut and seasonings. Heat thoroughly.

Roll out half of the dough on floured surface to ½ inch thickness. Cut in six 6-inch squares. Place 2 to 3 tablespoons meat mixture in center of each square. Fold over like ravioli and crimp edges with fork or fold corners to center; place folded side down on cookie sheet.

Repeat with remaining dough and meat mixture. Let rise until doubled in bulk.
Bake in 375 degree oven for 25—30 minutes or until golden.

BONUS: You can use *commercial* frozen bread. Let it rise, punch down and roll out—proceed as above. I think, however, you will prefer the bran bread.

The Kraut Bierocks can be served warm or room temperature. They are good *lunchers*. They also freeze very nicely.

OLD-FASHIONED BANANA BREAD

*Old-fashioned Banana Bread is one of several variations I have baked over many years of trying new recipes. This bread is more **bread-like** than **cake-like** - if you want Banana Cake—bake a cake and leave the **bread** in the Bananas if that's what your palate dictates...*

1 cup sugar
¹⁄₃ cup butter or
  vegetable shortening
5 or 6 tablespoons sour milk
  or buttermilk
2 beaten eggs
2¹⁄₂ cups all-purpose flour
¹⁄₂ cup chopped pecans
  or walnuts
3 small *black* (overly
  ripened) bananas
1 teaspoon baking soda
1 teaspoon lemon juice
1 teaspoon vanilla
Pinch of salt

Cream together the sugar and butter; add eggs and bananas (which you have *smashed* with a fork before adding to mix). Add 1 cup of the flour together with the baking soda (if using sour milk, add soda to the milk); add second cup of flour and vanilla and lemon juice. Mix the remaining ¹⁄₂ cup flour with the nuts and stir into batter.

Grease and flour large bread pan or two 9x5x2¹⁄₂-inch foil bread pans. Bake at 350 degrees for 45 minutes to 1 hour—if you use two smaller pans—it will be less than an hour—test with toothpick for doneness. Cool about 5 minutes and remove from pans to rack.

BONUS: I make up a *glaze* consisting of one cup powdered sugar, 1 teaspoon vanilla and a little milk to make a *thin frosting* - glaze with this while bread is still warm—it makes good bread better. I know you will like this added *baker's touch*.

HEATH AND HEATHER
SHORTBREAD

It is said that shortbread should be eaten while drinking Scotch whiskey—this does not appeal to my taste buds—but it seems to be a custom so observed on Hogmanay (New Year's Day) by the Scots. Whatever the custom, the following ingredients form a most delicious shortbread.

1 cup sweet butter, softened
½ cup granulated sugar
1 egg yolk
2 tablespoons thick cream
  (whipping cream)
1½ teaspoons vanilla
½ teaspoon fresh grated
  orange peel
2½ cups all-purpose flour
½ cup rice flour
  (I find this in our local
  health food store)

Cornmeal

Cream the butter and sugar in large mixer bowl—beat until light and fluffy; add egg yolk, cream, vanilla and orange peel—beat until blended. Combine the flours; work into the butter mixture and knead lightly—forming dough into a ball.

If you do not have a shortbread pan in your cupboard—read on.

Butter and flour an inverted 9-inch round cake pan. Press the dough onto surface to form a smooth circle. Sprinkle a baking sheet with cornmeal; invert dough circle onto baking sheet—you may have to loosen from cake pan at this point—using a spatula. Smooth top of dough. Using tines of fork, go around the edge of dough circle.

Bake in 325 degree oven for 10 minutes—at this point use a decorative shortbread or cookie press or butter mold and press design lightly in center. Also, score the shortbread in 8 wedges around the center design (use a pastry wheel or knife). Return shortbread to oven and bake another 30—40 minutes or just until edges begin to brown. Remove and cool on wire rack.

HUCKLEBERRY MUFFINS

If you live in an area where huckleberries are plentiful, try these muffins—they are so-o-o-o good. If you don't have huckleberries available to you—blueberries will suffice.

1¾ cups all-purpose flour
¼ cup sugar
1½ teaspoons baking
  powder
½ teaspoon salt
¾ cup milk
1 egg—well beaten
⅓ cup cooking oil
1 cup fresh—or frozen
  huckleberries, thawed
  and drained
3 tablespoons sugar
1 teaspoon grated lemon
  peel
1 teaspoon vanilla
½ teaspoon fresh grated
  nutmeg
Melted butter
Sugar

Mix together (by hand) the flour, ¼ cup sugar, baking powder and salt in large mixing bowl. Combine the milk, vanilla, egg and oil—add all at once to the dry ingredients, stirring quickly just until moistened. (Always use a light touch with muffins—overmixing will make a *tough* texture).

Gently mix the 3 tablespoons sugar with the berries and lemon peel. Again, fold lightly into batter.

Fill greased 2½ inch muffin pans two-thirds full.

Bake at 400 degrees for 20—25 minutes. While muffins are still warm, dip the tops in melted butter (not margarine), then in sugar.

Yield: 12

BONUS: You can use paper muffin liners if you prefer. Also, if you want to use miniature muffin tins—yield will triple.

FIT-AS-A-FIDDLE MUFFINS

*Not only are these muffins **fit for a Queen** - they are health-food fare—and good, to boot!!*

¾ cup butter
2 eggs
1½ cups sugar
1⅔ cups all-purpose flour
1½ teaspoons baking powder
½ teaspoon salt
1½ cups milk
1/3 cup wheat germ
1 cup currants (or raisins) (mix with a little of the flour above to keep from *globbing* into a bunch when you mix into the batter).

Cream together the butter, eggs and sugar in an electric mixer.

Stir into the butter mixture the flour, baking powder and salt— alternately with the milk (begin and end with milk).

Fold in with wooden spoon the wheat germ and currants (or raisins). Do not overbeat mixture—a few lumps will not *damage* the batter. By overbeating—muffins will become *tough*.

Fill paperlined muffin pan two-thirds full.

Bake in 375 degree oven for 25—30 minutes. Test for doneness.

Yield: 12 muffins

FRESH CRANBERRY NUT LOAF

This is a flavorful cranberry-orange nut loaf—good any time of the year—but especially appropriate during the Thanksgiving and Christmas season when fresh cranberries abound.

1¼ cups chopped cranberries
(Use blender or food
processor)
1 tablespoon grated
orange peel
2 tablespoons sugar
3 cups all-purpose flour
1 teaspoon baking powder
¾ teaspoon baking soda
¾ teaspoon salt
¾ teaspoon allspice
1¼ cups sugar
2 large eggs—beaten
¾ cup fresh squeezed
orange juice
½ cup water
¼ cup molasses
¼ cup melted shortening
½ cup chopped pecans

Combine cranberries, peel and sugar—set aside. Mix together the flour, baking powder, baking soda, salt, allspice and sugar. Mix beaten eggs with orange juice, water and molasses. Add to flour mixture together with the cranberries, shortening and pecans. Stir just until dry ingredients are blended.

Pour batter into a greased and floured 9x5x3-inch loaf pan. Bake at 350 degrees for one hour or until loaf is tested done.

Cool on rack for 15 minutes, remove from pan.

Drizzle orange glaze over the bread, cool completely and wrap in foil or plastic film overnight. Can be frozen.

BONUS: This recipe makes two smaller loaves—8x4x2-inches. Also— the bread can be frozen for gift giving or for later consumption.

ORANGE GLAZE:

Combine 1 cup sifted powdered sugar, ¼ teaspoon vanilla, 1 tablespoon fresh orange juice and enough milk to make glazing consistency (about 2 teaspoons).

FRESH RHUBARB LOAVES

*Particularly fragrant, somewhat likened to a banana loaf or zucchini bread are these Fresh Rhubarb Loaves. Hand out at breakfast, brunch, with soups, or just simply serve as a **between-meal** temptation.*

½ cup butter or margarine
1½ cups brown sugar
1 egg
1 cup buttermilk
2 cups all-purpose flour
1 teaspoon soda
½ teaspoon salt
1 teaspoon cinnamon
½ teaspoon freshly grated
  nutmeg
1 teaspoon vanilla
1⅓ cups finely diced
  rhubarb (food processor
  is easiest)
1 cup chopped pecans or
  walnuts

½ cup granulated sugar
1 teaspoon cinnamon

Cream together in a large mixer bowl the butter (or margarine), and brown sugar. Add the egg and beat until well blended. To the flour add the soda, salt, cinnamon, and nutmeg. With your mixer on low, combine the flour mixture alternately with the buttermilk. Blend in the vanilla. By hand stir in the nuts and lastly the rhubarb.

Pour batter into two greased and floured 9x5x2-inch bread pans. Sprinkle the mixture of ½ cup sugar and 1 teaspoon cinnamon on top of the unbaked loaves.

Bake in 350 degree oven for 40 to 50 minutes.

Remove from oven and cool completely before removing from pans.

BONUS: These rhubarb loaves are best the next day—the spices and rhubarb have a chance to *mesh*. Also, the bread can be frozen for later consumption.

LEMONY POPPY SEED BREAD

A nice, aromatic bread to serve with luncheon salads, soups or light dinners—especially if you thrive on poppy seeds.

¾ **cup sugar**
2 **eggs**
½ **cup milk**
½ **cup (1 stick) butter,**
  melted and cooled
2 **tablespoons fresh lemon**
  juice (or 1 tablespoon
  lemon extract)
1½ **cups all-purpose flour**
1 **teaspoon baking powder**
1 **teaspoon baking soda**
½ **teaspoon salt**
3 **tablespoons poppy seed**

Combine the sugar and eggs in large mixer bowl and beat until very light in color and *fluffy.* Slowly add the milk, butter and lemon juice/or extract. Blend well.

Add the flour—to which the baking powder, baking soda and salt have been added. By hand—add flour mixture and poppy seeds to the sugar and eggs. Turn the batter into a greased and floured 4x7 ½-inch loaf pan.

Bake in preheated 325 degree oven about 50 minutes or until bread is golden and tester inserted comes out dry.

BONUS: If you want more than one loaf, this recipe doubles nicely. Also— you will discover this to be a moist, cakelike bread. A nice accompaniment to a cup of tea or coffee.

WHEAT GERM ZUCCHINI BREAD

You will be pleasantly surprised with the result of this zucchini loaf. The unusual ingredients make a darker bread and add a bit of crunch to the unadorned, blasé species of zucchini creations.

3 eggs
1 cup salad oil
1 cup granulated sugar
1 cup brown sugar
3 teaspoons maple flavoring
2 cups shredded unpeeled
  zucchini
2½ cups all-purpose flour
½ cup toasted wheat germ
2 teaspoons baking soda
½ teaspoon salt
½ teaspoon baking powder
1 cup chopped walnuts
⅓ cup sesame seeds

Combine the eggs, salad oil, sugars and maple flavoring and blend. Add the flour, toasted wheat germ, baking soda, salt and baking powder. Mix well. Stir in zucchini and the chopped nuts.

Divide the mixture between two greased and floured 5x9-inch loaf pans. Sprinkle with the sesame seed.

Bake in a 350 degree oven for 1 hour.

BONUS: As all Zucchini breads—there is no exception here—it freezes beautifully.

ZUCCHINI BREAD PLUS

There are multitudinous recipes for Zucchini Bread, but this one is special in taste and texture. Family and friends will not turn down a second slice...

3 eggs, beaten
1 cup vegetable oil
2 cups sugar
2 teaspoons vanilla

2 cups zucchini coarsely
  shredded and unpeeled
1 — 8½ ounce can crushed
  pineapple—drained
3 cups all-purpose flour
2 teaspoons baking soda
1 teaspoon salt
½ teaspoon baking powder
¾ teaspoon fresh grated
  nutmeg (dig out that
  nutmeg grater)
1 cup chopped nuts
½ cup currants

Mix first four ingredients in a large mixer bowl and beat on medium speed until thick and foamy.

Stir in remaining ingredients. Grease and flour two 9x5-2 ½-inch loaf baking pans.

Spoon batter into pans and bake at 350 degrees for 45—60 minutes. Test at 45 minutes (toothpick will come out clean if done).

Yield: 2 loaves

BONUS: Freezing improves flavor!

PUMPKIN-CHIP BREAD

A very unusual combination of pumpkin and chocolate chips makes this loaf bread interesting and delicious. Kids love it, too!

1¾ cups all-purpose flour
1 teaspoon baking soda
1 teaspoon ground cinnamon
½ teaspoon fresh grated
   nutmeg
¼ teaspoon ginger
¼ teaspoon cloves
½ cup unsalted butter or
   margarine
1 cup sugar
2 eggs
¾ cup cooked (canned)
   pumpkin
1 cup chocolate chips
   (I like Nestles)
¾ cup chopped nuts
   (pecans or walnuts)

GLAZE:
½ cup powdered sugar
1 tablespoon milk
1/8 teaspoon freshly grated
   nutmeg
1/8 teaspoon cinnamon

Cream together the butter and sugar, blend in the eggs. Add dry ingredients (which have been combined)— alternately with the pumpkin— beginning and ending with dry ingredients. Fold in by hand the chocolate chips and ½ cup nuts.

Spoon into two greased and floured 9x5x2 ½-inch foil loaf pans. Sprinkle with remaining nuts.

Bake in preheated 350 degree oven for about 45—50 minutes. Test for doneness. Remove from oven, let cool 5 minutes. Remove from pans and *drizzle with glaze.* Best held overnight before slicing—this gives the spices a chance to *set in.*

Yield: 2 loaves

BONUS: Freezes well—if you are lucky enough to have a loaf *left over.*

SALADS:

SALADS:

Beef Super Supper Salad - 95
Best Fruit Dressing - 110
Bette's Caramel Apple Salad - 105
Blender Caesar Dressing - 111
Brenda's Strawberry Pretzel Salad - 109
Bridesmaids Delight - 103
Canlis' Special Salad - 98
Celebration Salad - 89
Coleslaw Souffle Salad - 92
Cranberry Fluff - 107
Dixie's French Dressing - 111
Dressed Artichoke Hearts - 100
Fresh Mushroom-Bacon Salad - 96
Frozen Mint Salad - 104
Grandma's Pineapple Salad - 102
Hot Chicken Salad - 94
Kari's Cabbage Plus - 93
Layered Lettuce Bowl - 90
Lora's Versatile Salad Dressing - 112
Marinated Combination Salad - 96
Marinated Mushroom Salad - 97
Matador Salad - 90
Micki's Chicken/Rice Salad - 94
Molded Waldorf Salad - 106
Mystery Salad Dressing - 112
Pepperoni/Garbanzo Salad - 91
Perl's Tabuli Salad - 92
Raspberry Creme Supreme - 103
Shoestring Salad - 100
Springtime Combination - 101
Strawberry Ring Mold - 108
Summertime Fruit Dressing - 110
Tomato Aspic - 99
Winter Fruit Bowl - 106

CELEBRATION SALAD

Is there a celebration in the offing? Celebration Salad will keep everyone jumping for joy.

4 heads broccoli
 (about 4 pounds)
2 large, firm tomatoes,
 cut into 3/4-inch cubes
2 tablespoons finely
 chopped purple onion

1¼ cups mayonnaise
1 tablespoon soy sauce
2 teaspoons fresh lemon
 juice
2 teaspoons seasoned salt
Salt
Freshly ground pepper

Lettuce leaves
2 hard-cooked eggs, chopped
½ cup unsalted roasted
 cashews
8 black olives

Trim broccoli and separate heads into flowerets. Steam broccoli until crisp-tender—about 5 minutes. Rinse in cold running water and drain in colander. Drain well and cool. Remove to a large salad bowl. Add tomatoes and onion tossing to combine. Refrigerate covered, until well chilled at least 2 hours.

Combine the mayonnaise, soy sauce, lemon juice and seasoned salt in small bowl. Set aside about ¼ cup. Gently toss remainder with the broccoli-tomato mixture. Add salt and pepper to taste; toss again.

Arrange lettuce leaves on individual salad plates; spoon salad into mounds dividing evenly. Sprinkle with the chopped egg and cashews. Spoon about 1 teaspoon of the reserved dressing on top of each salad. Garnish with an olive.

MATADOR SALAD

A similar salad first experienced at the Matador Hotel in Spokane, Washington—more years ago than I care to remember— however, the salad is memorable.

Salad greens (enough to
  fill a large salad bowl)
½ cup Parmesan cheese
4 strips cooked
  crumbled bacon
½ cup seasoned croutons

DRESSING:
Combine and shake well:
½ cup vegetable based
  salad oil
2 tablespoons white vinegar
½ lemon - juiced
1 egg - beaten
½ teaspoon fresh or
  dried parsley
2 teaspoons fresh or
  dried chives
1 sprinkling of garlic salt
  or powder (optional)
Dash of salt
A grind of pepper from
  the pepper mill

To a large bowl of salad greens add the Parmesan cheese and crumbled bacon. Toss with the dressing (about 20 tosses)—add the croutons and toss again. Serves six to eight—depending on how many *greens* you have utilized.

BONUS: This dressing is delectable with fresh spinach!

LAYERED LETTUCE BOWL

This is not only a very attractive addition to a dinner table—it can be layered the night before serving.

3 to 4 cups salad greens
  (variety of iceberg,
  curly endive, Romaine)

USING A CLEAR (CRYSTAL) GLASS BOWL, place half of the greens in bottom of bowl. Arrange the purple onion

1 cup purple onion rings—
thinly sliced
(one medium onion)
½ cup celery—cut in ½ inch
pieces on the diagonal
½ cup green or red bell
peppers, coarsely chopped
1½ cups fresh cauliflower
pieces
½ cup fresh broccoli
flowerets
1 package frozen peas
(thawed)
½ pound sliced bacon,
fried and crumbled
2 teaspoons dried Fines
Herbes (you can buy this
mixture of spices already
made up—it is not
hard to find)
1 cup salad dressing
(mayonnaise can be
substituted)
⅔ cup grated Parmesan
cheese (fresh is delightful)

slices around sides of bowl. Combine the celery and bell pepper in small bowl. Layer the cauliflower, broccoli, peas and celery mixture in that order over the greens. Sprinkle this with the bacon. Cover with remaining greens, sprinkling the Fines Herbes and pepper on top. Spread the salad dressing evenly over all and top with the Parmesan. Refrigerate—covered—8 hours or overnight.

BONUS: I use one 3 ounce can of "Crumbled Bacon—fully cooked and ready to use." There are several good brands on the market now and I find it easier to keep on the shelf than having to cook fresh bacon.

PEPPERONI/GARBANZO SALAD

The combination of pepperoni and garbanzo beans makes this a salad good with any Italian fare.

1 head lettuce
2 tomatoes - cut in wedges
1 cup Mozzarella cheese -
cubed
1 cup drained Garbanzo
beans
½ cup thinly sliced
pepperoni
6 sliced green onions
½ cup of your favorite
Italian style salad
dressing

Tear lettuce into serving pieces, add the remaining condiments and toss with an Italian dressing of your choice.

PERLE'S TABULI SALAD

An interesting salad, the original of which has been adapted from a recipe of the Canlis Restaurant in Seattle.

1 cup Bulgar wheat

Place in a bowl and cover with boiling water—let stand for 2 hours.

1 large tomato,
  peeled and diced
½ cup fresh parsley—
  snipped

Combine all of the ingredients. Store in jar in refrigerator. Use a tight lid on the jar. This will keep for a long time. Shake well before using.

1 teaspoon dried mint leaves
1 medium white onion—
  diced
½ cup imported olive oil
  (here's that olive oil again
  —I hope you have gotten
  the message by now)
¼ cup lemon juice
  (½ lemon squeezed)
1 teaspoon salt
Freshly ground pepper

TO SERVE: Tear Romaine into bite-size pieces and place in a salad bowl. Use just enough of a vinegar-oil combination to lightly wet leaves of the Romaine. Toss. Spoon some of the Tabuli mixture on top. When serving, be sure to get some of each of the Romaine and mixture.

Servings: You can determine how many this will serve by the size of portions you share.

COLESLAW SOUFFLÉ SALAD

This Coleslaw is in a soufflé form. It is a nice change from the American standard coleslaw!

1 tablespoon sugar
1 package unflavored gelatin
2 tablespoons water
1 cup hot water
½ cup cold water
2 tablespoons lemon juice
2 tablespoons vinegar
¼ teaspoon salt

SOAK gelatin in the 2 tablespoons water and add the one cup of hot water—stirring to dissolve the gelatin. Add½ cup cold water, the lemon juice, vinegar, mayonnaise, salt and pepper—beat until blended. Chill until nearly firm—beat until fluffy.

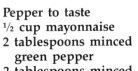
Pepper to taste
1/2 cup mayonnaise
2 tablespoons minced
   green pepper
2 tablespoons minced
   onion
2 cups shredded cabbage
1/4 teaspoon celery seed
1/4 teaspoon dill weed

Fold in the remaining ingredients and pour into a ring mold or individual molds. Chill until firm.

Serves 6-8

KARI'S CABBAGE PLUS

*If you are invited to bring a **buffet-style** salad—this is the one to take...*

1/2 head cabbage
   (not a huge one)—sliced
1 can tuna, shrimp or
   2 - 5 ounce cans chicken
2 tablespoons slivered
   almonds (toasted)
2 tablespoons sesame seeds
4 chopped green onions
1 package Ramen noodles—
   uncooked and broken
   apart

Dressing:
1/2 cup vegetable oil
3 tablespoons vinegar
2 tablespoons sugar
1 teaspoon salt
1/2 teaspoon pepper

Toss the above salad ingredients with the dressing at least three hours before serving. The Ramen noodles will soften.

BONUS: I use Garden Vegetable Flavor Top Ramen noodles. You could use whatever flavor you prefer.

MICKI'S CHICKEN/RICE SALAD

An elegant luncheon salad—this is one of the best and it is a pleasure to pass it on for others to enjoy.

5 cups cooked chicken—
  diced
2 tablespoons vegetable
  salad oil
2 tablespoons fresh
  orange juice
2 tablespoons vinegar
1 teaspoon salt

Combine and let rest while preparing the remainder of the salad—or—marinate overnight.

3 cups cooked rice
1½ cups small green
  seedless grapes
1½ cups diced celery
1 cup drained pineapple
  tidbits (13½ ounce can)
1 can mandarin oranges
  (11 ounce can drained)
1 cup slivered almonds
  (toasted)
1½ cups mayonnaise

GENTLY TOSS together—adding the marinated chicken mixture.

HOT CHICKEN SALAD

A delicious luncheon entree—called a salad—but actually is a very good hot dish.

4 cups cold cut up chicken
  (I like chicken breasts)
2 tablespoons lemon juice
⅔ cup finely chopped
  toasted almonds
¾ cup mayonnaise
1 teaspoon salt

Combine all but the cheese, potato chips and almonds. Place in large rectangular baking dish (9 x 11). Top with the cheese, potato chips and almonds. Let stand overnight in refrigerator Bake in 400 degree oven 20-30 minutes.

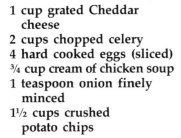

1 cup grated Cheddar
cheese
2 cups chopped celery
4 hard cooked eggs (sliced)
¾ cup cream of chicken soup
1 teaspoon onion finely
minced
1½ cups crushed
potato chips

Serves 8

BEEF SUPER SUPPER SALAD

Most definitely a Super Supper Salad—use up that leftover roast beef in this unusual combination. Guaranteed to be gobbled up by family or guests.

½ cup mayonnaise
1 tablespoon chili sauce
1 tablespoon sweet pickle
relish
¼ teaspoon salt

2 cups beef—cooked
and cubed
1—8-ounce can kidney
beans, drained (VanCamp's
New Orleans Style
kidney beans are tasty)
1 cup sliced celery
⅓ cup chopped onion
2 hard boiled eggs, chopped

Blend together the first four ingredients.
Combine remaining ingredients in a large serving bowl and pour dressing over all. Toss lightly and chill.

Yield—Serves four or five

BONUS: Salad can be doubled or tripled.

FRESH MUSHROOM-BACON SALAD

The perfect accompaniment to a barbecued or grilled steak.

12 slices bacon - cut
  in half inch pieces
  and cooked until crisp
3 green onions,
  sliced thinly
1 pound large fresh
  mushrooms - cut in
  quarter inch slices
Bibb lettuce

DRESSING:
²/₃ cup good imported
  olive oil
4 tablespoons fresh
  lemon juice
1 teaspoon Worcestershire
  Sauce
¹/₂ teaspoon salt
Twist of freshly ground
  black pepper
¹/₂ teaspoon dry mustard

Whisk everything together except the mushrooms, onion and bacon.
Pour dressing over the mushrooms and onion, cover and refrigerate for 5 hours. Stir occasionally.
To serve—with a slotted spoon, place mushrooms and onion onto a bed of Bibb lettuce, sprinkle bacon over all—use the remaining marinade to drizzle across the mushroom mixture.

BONUS: If you have not already come across my tip for olive oil, be sure to use a *good, imported oil* .

MARINATED
COMBINATION SALAD

Fresh mushrooms star in this marinated salad in combination with several other veggies. This is a good brunch salad as well as a salad to be served with any entree. It is especially good with Beef Wellington.

1 cup vegetable oil
2 teaspoons salt
2 teaspoons each dry basil
  and Dijon mustard

Combine the oil with the seasonings, vinegar and lemon juice. Blend with a fork until well mixed. At this point you can mix the marinade with all of

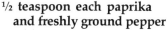

½ teaspoon each paprika
   and freshly ground pepper
5 tablespoons tarragon
   vinegar or white
   wine vinegar
4 teaspoons fresh
   lemon juice
2 pounds fresh mushrooms,
   sliced
Two bunches thinly
   sliced green onions
   (with some of the
   green tops)
1 small basket cherry
   tomatoes (stems removed)
1 large can pitted
   ripe olives
1 large can artichoke
   hearts, drained (or 2 jars
   marinated artichoke
   hearts, drained)
1 cup fresh broccoli
   flowerets

the veggies (except for the tomatoes) and marinate for about 1 hour at room temperature—stirring occasionally. Add tomatoes just before serving.
I frankly like the salad better when you refrigerate the dressing and the veggies separately and just before serving pour the marinade over all, toss gently and serve. This makes for a nice cool, *solid* texture. However, if you prefer a warm, marinated, *soft* textured salad the first instructions should be followed.

BONUS: You can double this nicely for a large crowd which I usually do—will serve 8-12 with *single* recipe and up to 20 when you double it.

MARINATED MUSHROOM SALAD

*A nice way to serve those big **white** mushrooms that are available in the Spring of the year.*

1 pound fresh mushrooms,
   coarsely chopped
2 tablespoons dehydrated
   onion flakes
2 teaspoons fresh
   lemon juice
½ teaspoon fresh
   ground pepper
½ cup whipping cream
¼ cup sour cream
2 teaspoons sugar
⅛ teaspoon dry mustard

Toss the mushrooms, onion, lemon juice, sugar and pepper in a glass bowl. Cover and refrigerate 30 minutes but no longer than 4 hours.
Whip the cream, folding in the sour cream, salt and dry mustard. Stir into the mushroom mixture.
Line a bowl with Romaine, mound the salad in center. Garnish with tomato wedges and fresh parsley. Serve immediately.
Serves 4-6

CANLIS' SPECIAL SALAD

*A wonderfully mild **Caesar-like** dressing makes this salad **special** - originated by Canlis' Restaurant in Honolulu, my friend March has enhanced it with her personal touch.*

1 head Romaine lettuce
1 fresh tomato—skinned

CONDIMENTS:
¼ cup chopped green onion (with some of the tops)
½ cup grated Romano cheese (freshly grated is best)
4-5 slices bacon cooked crisp and crumbled
1 cup croutons

DRESSING:
3 ounces imported olive oil
½ lemon—juiced
½ teaspoon fresh ground pepper
¼ teaspoon chopped fresh mint (dried will suffice if fresh is unavailable)
¼ teaspoon Oregano
1 coddled egg

USING A LARGE WOODEN SALAD BOWL—pour about 2 tablespoons olive oil—(Rob the piggy bank and buy yourself a bottle of *good imported olive oil* - it makes a world of difference in all recipes calling for it)—sprinkle with salt and rub firmly with a large clove of garlic. (The oil acts as a lubricant—the salt as an abrasive). Remove garlic and place the tomatoes cut in eighths, the Romaine which has been cut in 1-inch strips. You can add other veggies at this point—fresh broccoli flowerets are especially good—be sure to put the heavy vegetables in first—with the Romaine on top. ADD the condiments at this point.

DRESSING: In a bowl, pour the 3 ounces of *imported olive oil* , lemon juice and seasonings. Add the coddled egg and whip all vigorously. (A wire whip works great if you have one in your repertoire). When ready to serve the salad—pour dressing over, add croutons— toss. Serves six persons adequately.

BONUS: If you don't like the *bite* of a Caesar dressing—this is the salad for you—it is *most pleasurable* ...

TOMATO ASPIC

*To tell the truth, I **abhor** tomato aspic—simply because it will not go beyond my **uvula** (look that one up in the dictionary if you don't know what it means)..however, I am told that the following recipe is THE BEST of the LOT—so, if you **adore** aspic, please try this one!*

5 teaspoons unflavored
    gelatin
¼ cup cold water
2 cups tomato juice
⅛ cup sugar
1 teaspoon salt
⅛ cup lemon juice
    (fresh preferable)
1 dash each of:
    Salt
    Garlic salt
    Paprika
    Cayenne
¾ cup shredded carrots
⅛ cup sliced ripe olives
⅛ cup chopped walnuts

Soften the gelatin in cold water
Heat tomato juice, sugar and seasonings to boiling point.
Remove from heat and add the softened gelatin, stirring until dissolved.
Add:
    Lemon juice

CHILL UNTIL THICK AND SYRUPY

Add:
    Carrots, olives and nuts
Pour into a large decorative mold—a ring mold will suffice or you can use individual molds.

BONUS: That the aspic will be the best you have ever gotten past your uvula! ENJOY...

SHOESTRING SALAD

This salad could have been named after the saying "He lived on a shoestring" because it is inexpensive to make and satisfies that empty spot in the tum-tum.

1 cup chopped celery
1 cup shredded carrots
1 cup of any of the following:
  Shrimp
  Tuna
  Ham (bite-size pieces)
  Chicken (bite-size
    pieces), etc., etc.
1 cup salad dressing mixed
  with 1 teaspoon milk
  and 1 teaspoon sugar
¼ cup chopped onion
¼ cup toasted slivered
  almonds (optional)

Mix all of the ingredients and add:

1 can (2 cups) shoestring potatoes just before serving.

Serves four

DRESSED ARTICHOKE HEARTS

A quick, uncomplicated and tasty salad. Artichoke enthusiasts will be **thrilled.**

4 cups torn lettuce
8 cherry tomatoes—halved
1 - 9 ounce package
  frozen artichoke hearts

DRESSING:
½ cup oil
⅛ cup tarragon
  flavored vinegar
2 tablespoons water
4 thin slices of onion
1 clove garlic crushed
½ teaspoon salt

In a medium saucepan bring the *dressing* ingredients to a boil—add the frozen artichokes and cook just until tender. Pour all of this into a container and chill thoroughly. At serving time, drain, reserving the *dressing* . Toss with the lettuce, tomato halves and artichoke hearts. Serves six.

BONUS: If frozen artichoke hearts are unavailable in your area (as they are in mine), substitute a 14 ounce can of artichoke hearts which are readily

¼ teaspoon celery seed
Ground pepper (a couple
of turns on the pepper
mill—or a couple of
dashes of *table* pepper).

available (not the marinated ones—use
the artichokes canned in a water solution). Drain them, chill in the dressing which you do not have to cook,
and at serving time toss with the lettuce and tomatoes.

SPRINGTIME COMBINATION

*Spring seems to generate a **taste** for fresh fruits and garden veggies. This Springtime salad **combines** both.*

4 cups torn lettuce leaves
2 cups broccoli flowerets
1 cup sliced fresh
strawberries
2 peeled oranges - sectioned

DRESSING:
¼ cup honey
¼ cup vinegar
1 tablespoon poppy seeds
1 tablespoon sunflower
seeds (optional)
3 tablespoons fresh
lemon juice
1 tablespoon Dijon mustard
(do not substitute)
1 tablespoon finely
minced onion
⅛ teaspoon salt
⅔ cup vegetable oil

Combine the honey, vinegar, poppy seed, sunflower seeds, lemon juice, mustard, onion and salt in small bowl—whisk—gradually add the oil whisking or stirring until well combined.
Toss the lettuce, broccoli, strawberries and oranges in a salad bowl— a glass one shows off the colors—Pour dressing over all and toss lightly. Serves eight.

BONUS: Fresh pineapple chunks are a nice addition.

GRANDMA'S PINEAPPLE SALAD

*This is an old recipe—it may already be in your **favorites** file, but the only time it has been served to me has been at a relative's or in my own home. It is very simple to make.*

2 packages unflavored gelatin
1 cup cold water

(Soak the gelatin in the cold water for at least 30 minutes)

½ cup water
1 cup sugar

Boil these together until the mixture *threads* as for a cooked syrup for frosting, candy, etc. This should take about 5 minutes—or until it reaches softball stage on a candy thermometer. If you don't cook long enough, the salad will not *thicken*.

Add to the *thready* syrup mixture the gelatin which has been dissolving for a half hour. Pour the gelatin into the hot syrup — not the hot syrup into the cold gelatin—you will have a mess if you add the hot to cold...

Add one 8¼ ounce can of crushed pineapple, drained—stir to mix. Let all of this cool. I refrigerate about 15 minutes.

FOLD INTO THE COOLED MIXTURE:
1 cup of grated cheddar cheese
1 cup of whipping cream (whip)

This is best prepared in an 8 x 8 Pyrex dish or baking pan. Refrigerate until firm—at least 4 hours. Cut in squares and serve on bed of lettuce leaves. Serves 8

RASPBERRY CREME SUPREME

Raspberries are everyone's favorite —and this salad utilizes them especially well. It is a refreshing creation.

1 - 3 ounce package of
  Raspberry flavored gelatin
1 cup hot water
1 cup vanilla ice cream
3 tablespoons orange juice
1 - 9 ounce can crushed
  pineapple—drained
½ cup chopped pecans
1 banana sliced
1 - 10 ounce package frozen
  raspberries

Combine the first four ingredients. After partially thickened, add the remaining ingredients and chill until set.

You can use a 4 cup mold or 8 x 8 pan.

Serves 8 - 10

BRIDESMAIDS DELIGHT

I have no idea where the name originated, but the salad is delightful...

1 large can fruit cocktail
  (drain and save the juice)
½ pound marshmallows
¼ cup chopped nuts
½ pint whipping cream—
  whip, add a bit of
  powdered sugar and
  at least a teaspoon
  of vanilla
1 - 3¼ ounce box
  lemon pie filling
  (not instant)
1½ cups water
½ cup juice

Drain the fruit cocktail—save the juice
Mix together the fruit, marshmallows and nuts
Make the lemon pie filling, using the 1½ cups water and ½ cup of cocktail juice. Cool—using a cut glass or crystal serving bowl, mix the filling with the fruit mixture, fold in the whipped cream. Refrigerate the salad for several hours.

BONUS: Substitute a large can of *Fruit for Salad* for the fruit cocktail—the *chunks* are bigger and better..

FROZEN MINT SALAD

An amazingly simple salad to create—it is one of those all occasion, year-around treasures to share.

1 - 8¼ ounce can crushed
  pineapple
1 - 20 ounce can crushed
  pineapple
1 - 3 ounce package lime-
  flavored Jello
1 - 6½ ounce (3½ cups)
  miniature marshmallows
1 cup *Butter* mints
  (crushed) - these can be
  found in any grocery store
  - they are cream-colored
  and called *After-dinner
  Butter Mints*
1 - 9 ounce container
  (4 cups) dessert topping
  mix - thawed

In an oversized bowl combine the two cans of pineapple—DO NOT DRAIN—with the package of DRY lime Jello, marshmallows and crushed mints. Cover and refrigerate for 2-3 hours—or until the marshmallows start to get *soggy* and melt. To this—fold in the topping mix (Cool Whip). Spoon the completed mixture into 16 to 20 cupcake-paper lined muffin pans. Cover and freeze overnight. Peel off paper and serve on lettuce lined plates. If available, garnish with a fresh sprig of mint or if used at Christmas—add a maraschino cherry.

BONUS: These individual frozen salads can be kept in the freezer for at least a month. My friend Lora and I made about 200 of them for a *dinner* party and they *held* very well in insulated coolers for a couple of hours. We were not satisfied to use a *barrel* of wilted lettuce to feed our guests—and these little mint goodies were impressive as well as yummy!!!

BETTE'S CARAMEL APPLE SALAD

*If you need a salad to feed a **crowd** - this is the one. The recipe comes from an **almost** life-long friend who now lives in Indiana.*

1-20 ounce can crushed
pineapple
4 cups miniature
marshmallows
½ cup sugar
1 tablespoon cornstarch
1 egg—well beaten
1½ tablespoons
white vinegar
1 - 8 ounce Cool Whip
(room temperature)
2-3 apples
(diced, with skins)
1 cup Spanish salted
peanuts chopped
(remove skins)

Drain the pineapple, saving the juice. Mix the pineapple and marshmallows — set aside.

In medium saucepan, combine:
Cornstarch
Sugar
Egg
Vinegar
Pineapple Juice

Cook until slightly thickened over medium heat; cool and combine with the Cool Whip (which is at room temperature). FOLD in the marshmallows and pineapple mixture.

ADD the apples and peanuts.
This will *fit* nicely in a 9 x 12 pan. The salad should be refrigerated at least 8 hours—best if held overnight.

BONUS: I have used salted *cocktail* peanuts in place of the Spanish peanuts which you have to skin—it's much easier and I didn't find the taste or texture any different.

MOLDED WALDORF SALAD

*Here's a salad elegant enough for entertaining important guests and at the same time rates high on the family's **favorite** list.*

1¼ cups diced UNPEELED
  apples (Granny Smith's
  are good)
⅛ cup minced celery
  (diced very fine)
½ cup miniature
  marshmallows
1 - 3 ounce package
  mixed fruit gelatin
  (or any other flavor)
1¾ cups water
4 teaspoons lemon
  juice
¼ teaspoon salt

DRESSING:
1 cup mayonnaise
3 to 4 teaspoons
  sherry wine or
  orange juice
3 tablespoons chopped
  walnuts or pecans

Dissolve gelatin in 1 cup boiling water. Stir in remaining ¾ cup water, lemon juice and salt. Chill until syrupy—not completely thickened. FOLD in the diced apples which have been combined with the celery and marshmallows.

Pour into a one quart mold—or individual molds. Chill until firm. If using molds, remember to brush with a little mayonnaise to ease unmolding process.

UNMOLD and serve with dressing made by combining:
  Mayonnaise
  Sherry wine or orange juice
  Chopped nuts
Serves 6-8

BONUS: If using the salad on a buffet table, use a one quart ring mold—put the dressing in the center of ring for serving. If used as individual molds, use the dressing to *frost* the salads.

WINTER FRUIT BOWL

A particularly tasty combination of fruits—and excellent with a brunch menu.

4 medium pink grapefruit
1 cup granulated sugar

Pare and section the grapefruit—reserving the juice. Set the sections of

½ cup orange marmalade
2 cups (8 ounces) fresh or
frozen whole cranberries
4 small bananas

grapefruit aside.
To any juice from the grapefruit add enough water to make one cup. Combine this with the sugar and marmalade. Heat to boiling, making certain the sugar dissolves. Add the cranberries, stirring until you hear the skins pop—about 5 minutes. Remove from heat and cool.
Add the grapefruit sections, cover and chill. Just prior to serving, slice bananas and stir in the grapefruit mixture. Serves 10-12 nicely.

BONUS: A bit of freshly grated nutmeg and a sprinkling of coconut is a pleasant variation.

CRANBERRY FLUFF

*Cranberry Fluff is a **mahvelous** Thanksgiving or Christmas salad to serve with that turkey or ham.*

4 cups raw ground
 cranberries
6 cups miniature
 marshmallows
1½ cups granulated sugar

MIX THE THREE INGREDIENTS AND CHILL OVERNIGHT

NEXT DAY—
before serving, add:
4 cups diced unpeeled,
 tart apples
1 cup seedless
 green grapes
1 cup chopped pecans
 (or walnuts)
¼ teaspoon salt

FOLD two cups of whipped cream into the above - creating the *Fluff*. Serves 8-10.

BONUS: Serving the colorful *Fluff* in a crystal bowl is a must, obviously! This recipe can be easily halved.

STRAWBERRY RING MOLD

1 - 3 ounce package
  strawberry flavored Jello
½ cup boiling water
1 - 10 ounce frozen
  strawberries (drained)
1 - 10 ounce can pineapple
  chunks (drained) cut in
  two 2 bananas (sliced)
½ cup pecans - chopped
½ pint commercial
  sour cream

DISSOLVE the Jello in water

ADD - all ingredients EXCEPT the sour cream—and NO JUICES

POUR one-half of the strawberry mixture into a ring mold and congeal. Keep the other half of the strawberry mixture at room temperature. Spread sour cream on top of the congealed half and spoon the remainder of the strawberry mixture on top of the sour cream—you should then have a ring mold filled:
1. STRAWBERRY MIXTURE
2. SOUR CREAM
3. STRAWBERRY MIXTURE
Refrigerate until well congealed. To serve, unmold and fill center of ring with cottage cheese, fruit, etc. Serves 8 generously.

BONUS: Doubling the recipe makes a thicker and nicer ring mold. I don't quite double the sour cream—perhaps one-fourth more. Be sure to brush your ring mold with a little mayonnaise to make the unmolding a pleasant happening.

BRENDA'S
STRAWBERRY PRETZEL SALAD

A most refreshing fruit/Jello combination. It is particularly tasty with the fresh strawberries.

¾ cup margarine
3 tablespoons brown sugar
2½ cups crushed pretzels
(with a little substance—
not too crushed)
1 large package (6 ounce)
Strawberry Jello
2 cups boiling water
3 cups chilled fresh or
1 pound package of
slightly thawed
strawberries

1-8 ounce package cream
cheese (room temperature)
1 scant cup granulated sugar
1-8 ounce package Non-dairy
whipped topping
(Cool Whip)

Combine the margarine, brown sugar, semi-crushed pretzels—mix well. *Pat* this into a lightly buttered 9 x 13 pan and bake at 350 degrees for 15—20 minutes (until glowingly browned— as a graham cracker crust). COOL.

DISSOLVE Jello in the boiled water While still hot—add the strawberries, cool until mixture starts to set—it should set up quickly.

CREAM together the cream cheese, granulated sugar—carefully fold in the whipped topping (Cool Whip). Spread this mixture evenly over the crust which has cooled sufficiently.
Pour the partially set Jello and strawberry mixture over the top of the cream cheese layer. Refrigerate until firm—at least 8 hours or overnight.

BONUS: ENJOY this as a refreshing summertime dessert.

BEST FRUIT DRESSING

Definitely a fruit salad dressing at its BEST!

3 eggs—slightly beaten
¼ cup orange juice—
   Fresh preferred
¼ cup lemon juice—
   fresh preferred
¼ cup unsweetened
   pineapple juice

1 cup sugar
2 tablespoons flour

½ cup whipping cream

Blend the first four ingredients in top of a double boiler; add the sugar and flour mixture gradually into the egg mixture—STIRRING CONSTANTLY until thickened (this should take about 10 minutes). Cool and chill.

Before serving—whip the cream and fold into the cooked mixture.

BONUS: This is excellent with a fresh fruit bowl or gelatin salad.

SUMMERTIME FRUIT DRESSING

Refreshing is this easy and tasty favorite!

⅓ cup honey
⅓ cup vegetable salad oil
⅓ cup frozen limeade
1 teaspoon celery seed

Combine all of the ingredients—blending well. Serve over succulent fresh fruits. It is especially nice over sliced cantelope either for breakfast or served as dessert with a *Best of Friends, Etc.* Sugar Cookie.

BONUS: Triple the recipe and utilize the entire can of limeade—the dressing will keep very nicely in the *fridge.*

DIXIE'S FRENCH DRESSING

Actually, this is Dixie's Mother's French Dressing. It is a pleasant diversion from the basic **French Dressing** *served everywhere.*

1 cup salad oil
½ cup catsup
½ cup sugar
1 teaspoon salt
¾ cup vinegar
½ medium onion—ground

Combine and refrigerate.

The dressing separates easily so shake well before serving or mix in blender (Dixie says *my mother wouldn't*)—but I, too, prefer the *blender-mixed* version.

Yield: 2½ cups

BLENDER CAESAR DRESSING

A super topping that complements any tossed salad. The dressing can be made ahead and it keeps well refrigerated.

1 egg—beaten
½ vegetable salad oil
1 clove minced garlic
  (or a couple of shakes
  of garlic powder)
½ cup parmesan cheese
¼ cup fresh lemon juice
1 teaspoon Worcestershire
  sauce
½ teaspoon salt
½ teaspoon pepper
  (or 4 twists of the
  pepper grinder)

Mix all of the ingredients—pour into a blender and let it *whir* until well blended.

BONUS: Keeps well in refrigerator. Put in a jar with a tight fitting lid. If you have fresh parmesan—it enhances the dressing.

LORA'S VERSATILE SALAD DRESSING

*Truly a versatile dressing—it adds interest to any **green** salad and is magnificent as a coleslaw dressing—let your imagination go rampant!*

½ cup sugar
1 teaspoon dry mustard
1 teaspoon salt
¾ teaspoon pepper
¾ teaspoon paprika
1 tablespoon Worcestershire
½ cup vinegar
½ cup vegetable salad oil
1 shake garlic salt or powder

Blend all of the above in a container with a lid. Refrigerate. The dressing will last up to three weeks in the refrigerator.

BONUS: Add a can of tomato soup and it becomes a great French dressing.

MYSTERY SALAD DRESSING

*Definitely a mystery recipe—I have it in my files in shorthand notes—it is an unusual and different dressing. It makes a full quart so you could have a **mystery dinner party** and have enough to make a gigantic salad...*

1 small bottle catsup
½ small bottle of A-1 sauce
¼ bottle Heinz 57
½ bottle worcestershire
½ cup vinegar
½ cup vegetable oil

Blend all of the ingredients and keep refrigerated.

SOUPS:

SOUPS:

COLD BERRY SOUP

*Beautiful to look at, and fun to serve as a **starter** for a luncheon or dinner. Bring out your prettiest wine glasses!*

2 cups strawberries, hulled, washed and put through a sieve. (I use my food processor and then put through a strainer. Basically what you need to do is to *juice* the strawberries and leave the seeds behind).

½ cup sugar
½ cup sour cream

Stir until well blended

Add and blend:

2 cups ice water
½ cup red wine

Correct the sweetening, if necessary. CHILL.

Serve in wine glasses.

Yield: Depending on strawberries — about 4 cups

BONUS: Add a fresh stemmed strawberry for garnish.

OLD-FASHIONED BEAN SOUP

Serve this as a Sunday evening meal for guests. It boasts a variety of beans, ham and seasonings. Don't let the length of the recipe deter you—it's not as difficult as it looks. Try it—you'll be glad you weren't dissuaded...

4 cups beans (make up a variety such as Pinto, Navy, Lima, split pea, lentil, kidney—a good way to clean out your cupboard)

Wash and drain the beans and peas.

In a large stock pot add:
The washed and drained beans and peas
3 quarts water
2 tablespoons salt
1 Ham hock (or a leftover ham bone)
*1 tablespoon Bouquet Garni (wrap in a little cheese cloth bag or put in one of those *Mesh seasoning balls* that you can purchase from any kitchen/cookware department store)

Simmer covered for 2½ hours.

Add:
1 large can undrained tomatoes
1 medium onion, chopped
6 stalks celery, sliced

Simmer uncovered 1½ hours until creamy
Add ½ cup red table wine and ¼ cup fresh or dried parsley

Yield: 10 *healthy* servings

BONUS: The soup ages well and is best when served the next day. Also, any leftover soup freezes well.

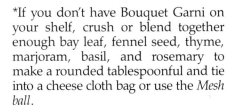

*If you don't have Bouquet Garni on your shelf, crush or blend together enough bay leaf, fennel seed, thyme, marjoram, basil, and rosemary to make a rounded tablespoonful and tie into a cheese cloth bag or use the *Mesh ball*.

LENTIL SOUP

Flavorful and nourishing - etc. etc.

4 slices bacon - diced
¾ cup diced carrots
¾ cup diced celery
¾ cup diced onions

In a large stock pot or soup pot, add 3 ounces salad oil. Add the first four ingredients to the oil and saute until onions and celery are transparent. Stir frequently to keep from sticking and burning.

¾ cup flour

Add to mixture and blend well.

3½ cups water

Add water slowly - stirring constantly.

1 cup lentils
2 teaspoons salt
2 teaspoons seasoned salt
4 tablespoons beef base
    (or 4 beef bouillon cubes)
Pinch of nutmeg
    (fresh grated is superb)
1 twist of the pepper mill
¾ cup diced potatoes

Add all remaining ingredients and simmer for 3 hours. Stir occasionally to prevent lentils from sticking to bottom of pot.

Yield: 4-5 quarts

BONUS: Especially good served with the Lentil Soup is a crusty sourdough bread.

CHEESE & BEER SOUP

Smooth, savory and prepared with ease.

½ cup butter
1 cup flour
2 cans (13 ¾-ounce)
   chicken broth
1½ cups half and half
1—16-ounce jar processed
   cheese spread
6 ounces beer
1 tablespoon Worcestershire
   sauce
1 tablespoon chopped chives
   (fresh snipped are
   most flavorful)
Dash yellow food coloring

Melt the butter in a stock pot. Add the flour stirring until well blended. Heat over low heat five minutes, stirring constantly.

Gradually add the chicken broth and half and half. Mix until smooth and thickened.

Add the jar of cheese spread, mixing well until cheese is melted and soup is smooth.

Add the beer, Worcestershire sauce, chives and dash of yellow food coloring.

Cover and simmer on low heat 10—15 minutes. Stir frequently.

Yield: 6 servings

IRISH POTATO SOUP

Duo talents conspired to come up with a superfluous potato soup!

1 cup butter
3 cups water

6 medium white onions,
   thinly sliced (a food
   processor thin-slicing disc
   to the rescue)
10 baking-size potatoes,
   peeled and cubed
3 quarts—half-and-half milk

Melt butter in the 3 cups of water. Add onions and potatoes. Simmer, covered until very soft. Mash with potato masher and add the half-and-half.

Season to taste with garlic powder, dried parsley, salt and pepper.

Serve in individual soup bowls and garnish with fresh parsley.

Yield: Enough to serve a crowd!

GARDEN TOMATO SOUP

Tomato soup like no other you have experienced. This recipe is adapted from a Spokane, Washington recipe—the original of which calls for about three buckets of tomatoes, etc. I have utilized the basic ingredients so that you can savor the fruits of the harvest.

36 ripe tomatoes (skins removed and quartered)
⅓ bunch celery with leaves, chopped
½ green pepper, chopped
5 medium onions, chopped (If you have a food processor—use it to chop the celery, pepper, onions)

1 tablespoon dried parsley
3 whole cloves
1 bay leaf
8 - 10 whole peppercorns
¼ teaspoon crushed red pepper flakes (optional)

BUTTER SAUCE:
⅓ pound butter
⅓ cup salt

BROWN SUGAR PASTE:
½ cup brown sugar
1 cup flour

Put all of the ingredients in a large kettle.

Cook until celery is soft; then add the Butter Sauce and Brown Sugar Paste.

Mix the sugar and flour together. Add enough of the hot soup to make a paste, then stir this into the hot soup and bring to a boil until soup thickens.

If the soup is thicker than you prefer, add a little water—I personally do not like it so thick. By adding the red pepper flakes I found the soup *zingier* - it can be too sweet, depending on the tomatoes.

Yield: 6 - 7 quarts—depending on size of tomatoes.

BONUS: Soup may be put in hot jars and processed in hot water bath according to any canning book directions—15 minutes at least—or soup can be put into plastic freezer containers and frozen. It keeps well either way.

Warn partakers of this soup not to bite into a peppercorn—for obvious reasons.

SALLY'S SEAFOOD GUMBO

An elegant Gumbo, serve as a dinner entree with a fruit and/or green salad and **huckleberry** *muffins. It makes my palate* **squiggle** *thinking about it.*

2 quarts seafood stock
16 crab claws
3 cups diced onion
2 cups diced green pepper
1 - 16 ounce can whole
  tomatoes, undrained
1 cup tomato puree
3 tablespoons gumbo *File*
  (get at fish market,
  or meat market)
2 - 10 ounce packages frozen,
  uncut okra (do not thaw)
¼ cup Creole seafood
  seasoning or to taste
  (I use about ⅛ cup and
  it is plenty *sharp* -
  I suggest you start out with
  a tablespoon and add more
  if you like it really *hot.*

1½ teaspoons saffron threads
4 bay leaves
½ teaspoon salt
30 large shrimp, raw,
  peeled and deveined
  (about 2½ pounds)
24 fresh oysters (optional)
1 pound lump crabmeat

Combine the stock, onion, green pepper, tomatoes and tomato puree in large stock pot. Bring to a boil over medium heat. Simmer 10 minutes.
Add all other ingredients and simmer another 10 minutes.
Add seafood and continue cooking an additional 10 minutes.

Serves 10 - 12

BONUS: If you don't have fish stock on hand, you can substitute chicken broth. Also, depending on what kind of seafood is available in your area, you can substitute. I use scallops, clams and lobster instead of the fresh oysters and lump crabmeat. This is an expensive chowder to make, but really makes an elegant dinner.

I like to serve *Blum's Coffee Toffee* pie and espresso to make the evening total elegance!

CREOLE SEAFOOD
SEASONING:
⅓ cup plus 1 tablespoon
  salt
⅓ cup plus 1 tablespoon
  paprika

⅓ cup cayenne pepper
¼ cup black pepper
¼ cup granulated garlic salt
3 tablespoons granulated
  onion
2 tablespoons thyme

Keep in a jar for future use.

MINESTRONE SOUP

Chock-full of flavor-packed vegetables and seasonings makes this particular Minestrone a favorite among soup lovers.

½ cup dried pinto beans
2 slices bacon, diced
1 cup zucchini, unpeeled
  and diced
½ cup diced peeled eggplant
½ cup chopped leek
2 teaspoons fennel seed
¼ cup chopped onion
¼ cup diced celery
1 diced carrot
8 cups beef or chicken broth
  (homemade if you have it)
½ cup dry white wine
1 tomato—peeled, seeded
  and chopped
½ cup peeled diced potato
1 teaspoon tomato paste
½ cup pasta
¼ cup chopped fresh parsley
1 tablespoon basil leaves
¼ teaspoon dried oregano
  leaves
Salt and freshly ground
  pepper

Soak the beans in cold water—enough to cover—at least 6 hours or overnight.

Next day, drain the beans well and transfer to small saucepan. Cover with cold water and bring to a boil over medium heat. Reduce the heat and simmer until tender. Drain and hold aside.

Saute the bacon in Dutch oven over medium heat. Add the zucchini, eggplant, leek, onion, celery and carrot. Saute the vegetables until softened. Stir in the stock, wine, tomato, potato and tomato paste and bring to boil. Add seasonings. Reduce heat and simmer 30 minutes. Add the beans and pasta and simmer until heated through.

Yield: 8 servings

NEW ENGLAND CLAM CHOWDER

Creamy, easy to fix clam chowder—with plenty of clams for all!

3 - 7½ ounce cans
  chopped clams
6 ounces salt pork, minced
4 cups diced potatoes
1½ cups water
½ medium onion, chopped
2 cups milk
3 tablespoons all-purpose
  flour
1 cup half and half
1½ teaspoons salt
Fresh ground pepper—
  to taste

Strain the liquid from clams, reserving ½ cup.
In saucepan, fry salt pork until very crisp; remove and set aside. Add reserved clam liquid, potatoes, water and onion to drippings in pan. Bring to boil, cover and simmer until the potatoes are fork tender—15 - 20 minutes.
Stir in clams.
Blend ¼ cup of the milk into flour, then blend into remaining milk. Stir into the chowder together with the half and half and cook, stir until boiling. Add salt and pepper and sprinkle reserved pork bits on top.

Serves 6

BONUS: *Molded Waldorf Salad* adds color and harmony to this chowder.

MANHATTAN CLAM CHOWDER

*Here's the **other side of the chowder** - Manhattan style and my pick of the **litter** ...*

3 - 7½ ounce cans chopped
  clams
5 slices bacon,
  finely diced
1 cup finely chopped celery
1 cup finely chopped onion
1 - 16 ounce can tomatoes,
  chopped, undrained

Strain liquid from clams and reserve ½ cup. Partially cook diced bacon. Add celery and onion. Saute until soft. Add the clam liquid, and all other ingredients except the clams and 2 tablespoons cold water and flour.

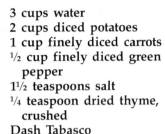

3 cups water
2 cups diced potatoes
1 cup finely diced carrots
½ cup finely diced green
  pepper
1½ teaspoons salt
¼ teaspoon dried thyme,
  crushed
Dash Tabasco

2 tablespoons cold water
2 tablespoons all-purpose
  flour

Cover and simmer 40 minutes.

Blend the flour into the cold water and add some of the hot chowder to make a paste. Return it to the chowder, stirring until well blended. Bring to a boil and simmer another 5 to 8 minutes.

Add the clams and heat through.

Serves 6 - 8

E-Z HAM CHOWDER

An E-Z way to make ham chowder utilizing any leftover ham you may have on hand or you can purchase enough in a local Deli to complete the ham portion of the chowder.

1 large onion
3 tablespoons butter

2 medium potatoes—cubed
1 cup water

3 tablespoons flour
½ cup water
3 cups milk
Salt & Pepper (to taste)

1½ cups cooked, cubed ham
1½ cups cubed pasteurized
  cheese spread (Velveeta)

Saute the onion in the butter, add the flour to onions. Add the onion to the potatoes which have been cooked in the 1 cup of water—do not drain the potatoes—add the remaining ingredients, heating until the cheese melts.

Yield: Six generous one cup servings.

BONUS: The refreshing *Cranberry Fluff* salad is good with the Chowder.

MOM'S HAMBURGER-VEGETABLE SOUP

A hearty combination of meat and vegetables makes this a meal in itself—not unlike a stew!

1 pound lean ground beef

1 cup of each of the following:
    Chopped onion
    Chunked Potatoes
    Thinly sliced carrots
    Shredded cabbage
    Sliced celery

1 - 32 ounce can tomatoes
¼ cup rice
3 cups water
4 teaspoons salt
¼ teaspoon basil
¼ teaspoon thyme
1 bay leaf

Brown the ground beef and onion together until *pink* has left the meat and it is lightly browned. Drain off any excess fat. Add all remaining ingredients and bring to a boil. Cover and simmer one hour.

BONUS: The soup can be accompanied with thinly sliced *Old-fashioned Banana Bread* or *Zucchini Bread Plus*.

VICHYSSOISE

Some like it hot! However, Vichyssoise technically is served cold. Whatever the choice may be—this brandy-laced potato soup is appealing to all.

6 potatoes, peeled
6 tablespoons butter
1 cup chopped onion
1 cup chopped celery
2—13 ¾-ounce cans
  chicken broth
4 cups half-and-half
2 cups diced boiled ham
½ cup chopped parsley
1 teaspoon salt
¼ teaspoon nutmeg
  (fresh ground)
¼ teaspoon white pepper
2 to 4 tablespoons brandy
  (optional)

Steam the potatoes in 1 inch of boiling water for 30 minutes or until tender. Cut into half-inch cubes. In large saucepan, melt the butter and saute onion and celery until tender.

In bowl of food processor or electric blender, combine 2 cups cubed potatoes, onion, celery and chicken broth. Process on high speed until smooth. Return to saucepan.
Add half-and-half, the remaining potatoes, ham, parsley, salt, nutmeg and pepper. Bring just to a boil. Reduce heat and simmer, uncovered for five minutes, stirring occasionally.

Just before serving, stir in the brandy.

Yield: 8 servings

B.W.'S BIRTHDAY SOUP

Scrumptious, easy to concoct, and a great birthday luncheon entree!

1 onion chopped
2 tablespoons basil
(fresh if available)
3 cans Cream of Asparagus
soup, undiluted
1 20 ounce can quartered
tomatoes, (half drained)

2 10 ounce cans
Chicken Broth

Saute the onions and basil in 3 tablespoons butter until soft.

Combine the Cream of Asparagus soup and tomatoes. Pour into a blender or processor and blend until tomatoes are chopped smaller. Pour into a *soup pot* and add the two cans of Chicken Broth.

Heat and serve.

Yield: Serves 8 - 10

BONUS: For garnish, leave out a few pieces of the tomato; cut them in half and place on top of soup before serving.

Fresh spinach greens with *Lora's Versatile Salad Dressing* would be a great accompaniment.

BLACK BEAN SOUP

*An especially spicy (Mexican style) soup. Don't let the **plain-wrapper** name fool you. This is not the run-of-the mill Navy bean soup—so read the ingredients carefully and if they tickle the **palate** - get out the soup kettle!*

1 **pound dried black beans**
2 **quarts of water**
6 **slices bacon, finely chopped**
1 **pound onions, finely chopped**
1 - **or 2 canned jalapeno chilies, drained, seeded and chopped**
1 **teaspoon garlic salt**
1 **tablespoon dried oregano leaves**
1 **tablespoon ground cumin**
¼ **cup water**

Jack cheese—shredded— for garnish

Rinse beans under water; drain and combine the beans and 2 quarts of water in soup kettle. Simmer covered until the beans are tender, stirring once in awhile and adding more water as necessary to keep beans from sticking to the bottom of the pot. (About 4 hours)

Lightly brown the bacon in a skillet over medium heat. Add the onions and jalapeno chili. Reduce the heat and cook until onions are soft— about 10 minutes. Add the onion mixture to the beans. Stir in the cumin and oregano, simmer 30 minutes—stirring occasionally. Check seasoning and add salt if desired.

Spoon soup into heated bowls and top with shredded Jack cheese

Yield: 6 to 8 servings

BONUS: If you have a hard time finding black beans, run to the nearest Health Food Store and you will find black turtle beans. I have never seen them in the local grocery store.

SATURDAY NIGHT CHILI

*Some people will tell you that there is only one way to make chili. However, chili is one of the most fun and creative dishes to experiment with and also basically **personal** . Let your ideas run rampant and **do your own thing**. BJ's Alpha Dough-Me's are great with the chili.*

This is my own thing:

1 pound lean ground beef
1 package commercial chili mix
½ medium white peeled onion, chopped

2 cans Van Camp New Orleans Style kidney beans (do not drain)
2 tablespoons chili powder
2 dried red chilies crushed or ½ teaspoon crushed chili flakes
2 teaspoons salt
¼ teaspoon ground cumin
1½ cups water
1 can stewed tomatoes (*smooshed -* don't leave chunky)
1 or 2 cups tomato juice— depending on how soupy you like your chili

Brown the beef in a tablespoon of vegetable oil, add the onions.

Add all other ingredients in any order you choose. Simmer for about 1 hour.

Yield: 6—8 servings

BONUS: This chili freezes well; any leftovers can be utilized in an omelet or spoon over Freezer Burritos Bellingham.

ENTREES:

ENTREES:

Anniversary Crown Roast of Pork - 146
Applesauce-Baked Stuffed Pork Chops - 143
Beef Enchiladas - 164
Beef Wild Rice Casserole - 151
Betty's Favorite Lasagne - 170
Burnham's Bloomsday Spaghetti Sauce - 168
Chicken Lasagne - 136
Chicken and Stuffing Casserole - 132
Chicken Divine - 133
Chimichangas - 166
Chinese Chicken - 137
Creamy Mexican Chicken Enchiladas - 163
Filet of Sole Bundles - 159
Flavorful Meatballs - 152
Freezer Burritos Bellingham - 165
Glazed Pork Roast - 144
Grilled Barbecued Pork Chops - 147
Honolulu Sauerbraten - 155
Italian Sherry Chicken - 135
Jose's Delight - 167
Lemon Shrimp Oriental - 156
Oven Crisped Trout - 161
P.K.'s Pleasant Pheasant - 138
Palm Springs Chicken - 131
Pasticcio - 171
Peking Roast - 149
Pheasant Urb - 139
Polynesian Fish - 162
Puebla Pork Roast - 145
Scampi - 158
Seafood Tetrizini - 158
Sesame Chicken - 134
Shrimp Au Gratin - 157
Shrimp & Scallops Swiss - 160
Skewered Beef - 153
Spaghetti Sauce with Distinction - 169
Spicy Pot Roast Veal - 139
Stuffed Hamburgers - 150
Tarragon Chicken Trieste - 134
Veal Oscar Supreme - 140
Veal Scallopini - 141
Vegetable/Steak Oriental - 148
Vienese Veal and Noodles - 142
Zesty Barbecued Ribs - 154

PALM SPRINGS CHICKEN

A delicious entree, serving 12 very adequately. The side dish **Wild Rice & Cashews** *is a tasty* **sidekick,** *served with a nice Reisling or Blanc de Blanc wine. A fresh fruit bowl will cover the remainder of the dinner. How about serving Coffee Mocha Nudge for dessert??*

¼ cup flour
2 teaspoons salt
1 teaspoon paprika
12 halved chicken breasts
(skinned and boned)
1 teaspoon cornstarch
1½ cups Half and Half
¼ cup cooking Sherry
(not for the cook)
½ package dry chicken broth
1 teaspoon grated lemon peel
1 tablespoon lemon juice
(2 are even better)
1 cup grated Swiss cheese
½ cup parsley (fresh-
chopped)—dehydrated
is acceptable)

Mix the flour, salt and paprika. Coat chicken with this mixture. Lightly brown the chicken (use vegetable oil, margarine, or butter). Add ¼ cup of water and simmer, covered for 30 minutes. Arrange the chicken in your fanciest *in the oven to the table baking dish.* Mix the cornstarch and ¼ cup of the Half and Half. Stir this into the drippings, cook over low heat, gradually stirring in the remaining Half and Half, Sherry, chicken broth, lemon peel and lemon juice. Cook, stirring until thickened—like a gravy—pour over the chicken.

Cover and bake at 350 degrees for 40 minutes.

Uncover, sprinkle the cheese and parsley (which you can mix together beforehand) on top of the chicken—return to oven just until the cheese melts—about 10 minutes.

You can serve these on individual dinner plates, unless you have used a real *impressive* baking dish to prepare the chicken in.

BONUS: You can cut this recipe in half if you don't plan to serve 12 hungry souls.

CHICKEN AND STUFFING CASSEROLE

An innovative chicken and stuffing main course with the stuffing on the outside.

5 cups dressing cubes
(commercial)
1 cup chopped celery
3 cups cooked chicken—
cut up in chunks or
small serving pieces
1 tablespoon minced
dry onion
6 eggs
3 cans condensed cream of
chicken soup
2 cups milk
1 teaspoon poultry seasoning
Salt and pepper
½ cup flour
¼ cup grated parmesan
cheese
¼ cup butter
Slivered almonds

Combine the bread cubes and celery in a buttered 3 quart casserole (9 x 13 baking dish is about the right size). Arrange the chicken over the cubes and celery and sprinkle with the onion.

Combine the eggs (slightly beaten with a fork), soup, milk, poultry seasoning and (salt and pepper to taste)—pour this over the chicken mixture.

Combine flour and cheese, cut in the butter. Sprinkle this over the above mixture and top with slivered almonds if desired.

BAKE at 375 degrees for 35 to 40 minutes—it is ready for serving when a knife is inserted in center and comes out unencumbered (no goodies on it).

BONUS: An impressive entree that can be made up the night before you need it. Layered Lettuce Bowl, Hugh Ford's Potato Rolls and Gen's Baked Chocolate Pudding superbly round out this menu.

CHICKEN DIVINE

Chicken Divine (Divan) can be found in almost everyone's reper-
toire of chicken dishes. This recipe is particularly good and I have
found it to be the favorite of many divan-lovers. **Caramel Apple**
Salad *is a pleasant* **accomplice** *with this curry-flavored dish.*

3 cups cooked chicken
(from chicken breasts)
2 packages frozen
broccoli spears (cooked)
2 cans Cream of
Chicken soup
1 cup mayonnaise
1/4 teaspoon curry powder
1 tablespoon lemon juice
1 cup grated sharp
cheddar cheese
4 tablespoons melted butter
1 cup crushed Ritz crackers

In a 9 x 13 casserole dish or other dish of equal capacity (a nice big Dansk casserole pan works beautifully) space the broccoli evenly. Place the chicken pieces (bite-size) over the broccoli.

MIX: Soup, mayonnaise, curry, lemon juice and pour over the above.

MIX: The crushed Ritz crackers and melted butter—scatter over all, add grated cheese and

BAKE—uncovered at 350 degrees for 30 minutes.
Serves 6—8

BONUS: This is an especially easy dish to create—I have made up ahead of time for large dinner parties. The *expert chefs* say not to freeze anything with mayonnaise in it; however, I have had good luck freezing the Chicken Divine, leaving the crumbs off until right before baking.

TARRAGON CHICKEN TRIESTE

*A **one-pan** entree which transforms itself into an elegant dinner for six. Matador Salad is an excellent accompaniment to this dish together with Celery Rolls in a Loaf and Sacked Apple Pie adorned with a scoop of vanilla ice cream.*

½ **pound fresh mushrooms**
¼ **cup butter**
6 **large boned chicken breasts**
2 **teaspoons Beau Monde seasoning**
½ **teaspoon tarragon**
1 **cup dry white wine (Chablis is perfect)**
1 **cup dairy sour cream**
½ **cup chopped green onions**

Slice the mushrooms and saute in 2 tablespoons of the butter just until golden. Remove from pan and reserve.

Add the remaining butter to pan and brown chicken well—sprinkling with the Beau Monde seasoning during browning process. Add the mushrooms, sprinkle with tarragon, and pour wine over the chicken.

Cover and simmer 45 minutes or until fork tender. Remove from pan and keep warm.

Spoon the sour cream into pan and heat (do not boil). Place the chicken breasts on serving platter, spooning the sour cream over all, and scatter the sliced green onions on top.

BONUS: If you grow fresh herbs at your house, use fresh tarragon— it's super delectable.

SESAME CHICKEN

Such an easy entree to prepare, but tastes like you spent all day in the kitchen working at it—No need to tell anyone differently.

Six boneless chicken breasts

Make a pocket in each chicken breast

Swiss cheese
Ham
Sesame seeds

and stuff with two pieces (½ x 3 inches) Swiss cheese and 1 piece of cooked ham the same size.
Brown the chicken in butter; brush with a mixture of 2 tablespoons melted butter and 1 tablespoon Soy sauce. Sprinkle generously with sesame seeds.

BAKE at 350 degrees for 35—45 minutes.

ITALIAN SHERRY CHICKEN

A well-seasoned chicken dish—a real treat for chicken enthusiasts!

Six pieces of chicken
(I prefer to use
chicken breasts)

Marinate the chicken in dry sherry for two hours—use enough sherry to cover the chicken. Drain and pat dry. Dip in beaten egg and then in seasoned bread crumbs. Brown the chicken in butter.
Place chicken in an oven-proof baking dish and pour the following sauce over it:

SAUCE:
1 small can tomato sauce
¼ teaspoon of each
  of the following:
    Sweet basil
    Marjoram
    Chili powder
    Oregano
    Parsley
⅛ teaspoon pepper
1 teaspoon sugar
1 teaspoon salt
Dash of Tabasco

SIMMER the sauce for 15 minutes

BAKE at 350 degrees uncovered for 30—40 minutes—until done Remove from oven, and top each piece of chicken with a slice of mozzarella cheese. Bake another 5 minutes or until cheese is melted.

CHICKEN LASAGNE

*A yummy lasagne **diversion** - if you are tired of serving **beef** sauce— Betty—this might be for you!*

COOK 8 ounces
lasagne noodles*
3 cups cooked diced chicken
(I use cooked chicken
breasts—saving the broth
for other recipes or just
plain old-fashioned
noodle soup)
2 cups shredded
American cheese
(I prefer sharp cheddar)
1½ cups cream-style
cottage cheese

SAUCE:
Saute in 3 tablespoons
of butter:
½ cup chopped onion
1 green pepper chopped

Stir in:
1 cup Cream of
Chicken soup
⅛ cup milk
1 - 6 ounce can mushrooms
1 small jar pimento,
chopped (definitely an
option if you don't
like pimento)
½ teaspoon Basil
(fresh, powdered or leaves)

LAYER in a 9 x 13 inch pan, using one-half the ingredients:
NOODLES
CHICKEN
SHREDDED CHEESE
COTTAGE CHEESE
SAUCE

REPEAT using the remaining ingredients

SPRINKLE with ½ cup parmesan cheese for a tasty finishing touch.

BAKE at 350 degrees for 45 minutes
Serves 8—10

BONUS: Can be frozen for baking later.

*TIP—Cook the noodles in salted water with 1 tablespoon vegetable oil for about 20 minutes. Remove from heat, drain off hot water, add cold water to the pan while preparing the lasagne—the cold water will keep the noodles from sticking together.

CHINESE CHICKEN

Called Chinese Chicken because of the Chinese noodles used in the formation of this crunchy chicken casserole.

6 large chicken breasts

Simmer the chicken breasts with 1 celery stalk, chopped onion (take a guess as to how much you want to use), and salt to season. I usually cook the chicken about an hour. Refrigerate the chicken overnight in the stock for most flavorful chicken—however, this is not absolutely necessary if you want to get on with the preparation.

Next day, remove chicken from the stock, bone and leave in large serving pieces.

Place in large bowl with the following:

1 can Cream of Celery soup
1 small can of mushrooms
(whole or bits and pieces)
2 cups mayonnaise
(not salad dressing)
1 package slivered almonds
1 can sliced chestnuts
3 tablespoons green onion—
sliced (this usually means
a small bunch of onions)
2 cups diced celery

Mix all of the above ingredients and turn into a buttered casserole.

Bake at 400 degrees for 30 to 40 minutes. Remove from oven and sprinkle with a can (2 ounces) of Chinese Noodles. Return to oven for a few minutes just until noodles are hot.

BONUS: This entree can be made up and divided into two smaller casseroles. Bake one for dinner and freeze the other one—if you freeze—do not put the Chinese Noodles on until you bake for serving. Chinese noodles do not freeze well—they become *mooshy* .

P.K.'S PLEASANT PHEASANT

*A real treat for those of us who are fortunate enough to have the luxury of pheasants in the field for **harvesting** ... Chicken can be used if pheasant is out of your reach. **Cranberry Relish Salad** and a Wild Rice dish is good with this.*

1 Pheasant
½ cup butter
(DON'T SUBSTITUTE)
1 pint heavy cream
(Whipping cream or
Cow-fresh if you're lucky
enough to have a source)
Salt and pepper

Cut up one pheasant and shake in a bag with flour, salt and pepper. In a large, heavy roaster, melt the butter. Slowly brown all of the pheasant on all sides—add more butter if necessary.

COVER and bake for 2 hours in a 300 degree oven.

TAKE out of oven and cool; slowly add the cream to the pheasant, cover the pan and put back in the oven for about another hour.
When done—you will have a truly elegant, succulent pheasant in its own creamy gravy.

BONUS: You can double or triple the recipe—use your best judgment when using more than one pheasant or chicken.

PHEASANT URB

An old recipe handed down in tack. Names may lend as much flavor as herbs.

6—8 pheasant breasts
¾ cup dry white wine
(I use a Chablis)
¼ teaspoon thyme
1 can cream of chicken soup
1 can mushrooms
1 can sliced water chestnuts
½ cup butter

Brown the pheasants which have been salted but not floured. Place in a shallow baking dish. Add the soup to the pan drippings and mix. Slowly add the wine, stirring in well and add all other ingredients, bring to a boil and pour over the pheasant.

BAKE covered at 350 degrees for 35 minutes; then uncovered at 325 degrees for 25 minutes.

SPICY POT ROAST VEAL

*A super way to serve a **cheaper cut** of veal (I don't really honestly know if such a **creature** exists). However, Spicy Pot Roast is delicious under any circumstances. Vegetable Melange would be a good vegetable side dish to serve with this roast along with Bette's Caramel Apple Salad. Don't forget that **sweet something** - Sally's Almond Lace Wafers—for dessert.*

3 pound veal roast
(for *potting*)

1 tablespoon dry mustard
1 teaspoon poultry seasoning
2 tablespoons flour
1 tablespoon brown sugar
1 tablespoon salt
Pepper

3 tablespoons shortening
1—2 cups red cooking wine
1 onion sliced
Garlic (to taste or omitted)

Mix together the flour and seasonings. Dredge the meat in the mixture and brown in a roaster pan with the shortening. When all sides are nicely browned, add the sliced onion and red wine. Cover and cook in a 350 degree oven for 3 hours.

Before serving—remove meat from pan and with any flour and spices remaining add to water and mix in the pan over medium heat for a delicious gravy to serve with the Spicy Pot Roast Veal.

VEAL OSCAR SUPREME

*An absolutely perfected method for preparing Veal Oscar. Definitely not a time consumer—it can be prepared quickly and without **fuss** or **muss**. Dressed Artichoke Hearts, Fit-As-A-Fiddle Muffins and Banana Cream Pie are suggested companions.*

4 to 6 veal cutlets,
    ¼-inch thick and
    pounded thin
3 tablespoons fresh
    lemon juice
Pepper
Flour seasoned with
    Seasoned Salt or other
    seasoning
18 spears fresh asparagus,
    cooked
4—6 crab legs, cooked
    and shells removed
1½ cups Hollandaise or
    Bearnaise sauce (See *Etc.*
    index)

Sprinkle the cutlets with fresh lemon juice and pepper (both sides). Dredge in seasoned flour.

Heat ¼ cup butter (more or less—depending on number of cutlets) in a large skillet. Saute cutlets over medium heat until lightly browned on each side—about 5 minutes. Remove to platter and keep warm. On each cutlet place 3 spears of the asparagus and one crab leg. Spoon Hollandaise or Bearnaise sauce across top of cutlet.

BONUS: The Bearnaise sauce is not so *overpowering* - so I prefer it. You can also use frozen crab—lump style—or canned crab—lump style—if the crab legs are not readily available in your area. My preference for white lump crab dictates how I serve the cutlets - you can use your imagination for other methods of utilizing the kind of crab you prefer. Also if fresh asparagus is not in season, frozen spears or canned asparagus tips work well.

VEAL SCALLOPINI

This veal entree has been in my files forever and when veal is available—no matter what the cost—I make scallopini. I have made the mistake on numerous occasions of ordering it from a menu while dining out. Once you have tasted this veal scallopini, don't order at a restaurant because you will not find one that prepares it as marvelously as this . . .

**3 pounds veal round steak—
(¼ inch thick)
3—4 tablespoons olive oil**

**½ cup chopped white onion
1 small clove garlic—minced
(optional)
1 cup dry Chablis or cooking
Sauterne wine
1—4 ounce can mushroom
caps and stems
1—15 ounce can tomato sauce
1 teaspoon thyme
1 teaspoon rosemary
½ teaspoon salt
¼ teaspoon pepper**

**1—10 ounce package tiny
frozen peas**

Cut veal in small serving pieces—1½ x 1½-inches.
Dredge in flour and in large pan, brown in olive oil. After all the scallops have been browned—add everything else except the peas. Simmer over low heat for 1½ hours—or until veal tests tender. Add the frozen peas and simmer just long enough to cook them.

For serving, spoon into large chafing dish and place on dinner table. It can be served with rice or buttered noodles as a side dish. Fresh spinach with Blender Caesar Dressing complements the veal and Fresh Apple Cake is a pleasant encore to this repast.

BONUS: Veal is not always available in my area, so when it is I buy enough to make a double recipe and freeze whatever might be left over. It freezes super—I just warm it up in the oven in a casserole dish—or if you are one of those who has a microwave it would heat nicely there. Have a go at it. I just know you will like Veal Scallopini.

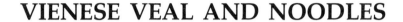

VIENESE VEAL AND NOODLES

A very subtle dish which cannot be ameliorated...Try Marinated Combination Salad, Fresh Strawberry Pie and a pot of fresh, hot espresso to end a memorable evening.

2 pounds veal round
(¼-inch thick)
6 tablespoons butter
2 cups light cream (Half and
Half works well)
3 teaspoons paprika
4 tablespoons poppy seeds
Garlic—1 clove

3 cups noodles—fine cut
½ cup parmesan cheese

Cut the veal into 1/2-inch squares
Brown in the melted butter with the garlic
Remove the garlic when meat is browned and add:

Half and Half
Paprika
Poppy seeds

Simmer over very low heat for 15 minutes. Keep heat low so that half and half does not boil away, but cooks down just a bit.

Cook the noodles in boiling, salted water. Drain and toss with the parmesan cheese. Place noodles in large serving dish, make a *well* in center and spoon the veal mixture over and into the well of the noodles.

BONUS: A nice Riesling wine is just the right touch with this entree.

APPLESAUCE-BAKED STUFFED PORK CHOPS

*Pork and apples are melodious—they naturally go hand-in-hand. Applesauce-Bake Stuffed Pork Chops are splendid **company fare**. Appealing **go-alongs** might be Festive Corn Bake and Sour Cream Apple Pie—don't forget lots of freshly brewed coffee or tea.*

6 double-rib pork chops
  with pockets
¼ teaspoon salt
½ teaspoon onion salt
1 cup bread stuffing
¼ cup hot water
2 tablespoons soft butter
1—16-ounce can applesauce
¼ cup water
¼ teaspoon salt
1/8 teaspoon each:
  Thyme, marjoram and
  oregano

Mix bread stuffing with hot water and butter; fill pockets in the chops with the dressing. (Use toothpicks to seal in the dressing). Season chops with the salt and onion salt. Arrange in a shallow casserole baking dish.

Combine applesauce, water, and salt. Pour the mixture over the chops and sprinkle with herbs.

Bake at 350 degrees for 1½ hours, covered.
Uncover and continue baking for 20 minutes more, basting occasionally.

Yield: 6 servings

BONUS: You can use your favorite dressing if preferable. Also, I brown the porkchops on each side before placing in casserole for baking. If you choose to do so—cut down about 10 minutes on the baking time.

GLAZED PORK ROAST

Grape glazed pork loin is a pleasant diversion. Broccoli with Cheese, Frozen Mint Salad and Rhubarb Surprise Pie are excellent tag-alongs with the pork—tried and true!

1 pork loin roast
 5 to 6 pounds
Salt and pepper
½ cup grape jelly
1 tablespoons cider vinegar
¼ teaspoon ground ginger

2 tablespoons cornstarch
¼ cup grape jelly
1½ cups water

Sprinkle the pork with salt and pepper and place on a rack in roasting pan. Insert meat thermometer so tip is in center and thickest part of meat and does not touch a bone. Roast in a 350 degree oven about 2½ to 3 hours or until thermometer registers 170 degrees.

Heat ½ cup grape jelly, the vinegar and ginger in a small saucepan over low heat, stirring constantly, until the jelly melts. An hour before the pork is done, baste pork every 15 minutes with the glaze.

Remove pork from pan.

Heat ¼ cup pan drippings in small saucepan over medium heat. Blend in the cornstarch and cook, stirring constantly until smooth. Add the ¼ cup grape jelly and the water. Cook, stirring constantly until thickened. Serve in gravy boat alongside the pork loin.

Yield: 8—10 servings

PUEBLA PORK ROAST

Celebrate Cinco de Mayo with this South of the Border spicy pork loin. Halved fresh avocados filled with a mixture of garbanzo and kidney beans go well with this entree. I also like Chocolate Sheet Cake squares to round off this spicy combo.

**4—5 pound boneless rolled
pork loin roast**
½ teaspoon salt
½ teaspoon garlic salt
1 teaspoon chili powder

GLAZE:

½ cup apple jelly
½ cup catsup
1 tablespoon vinegar
½ teaspoon chili powder
1 cup crushed corn chips

Combine the salt, garlic salt and ½ teaspoon chili powder. Place the roast fat side up on rack in a shallow roasting pan and rub the salt and chili powder mixture into the roast. Roast in 325 degree oven for 2½ hours or until meat thermometer registers 165 degrees. At this point glaze with the following:

In a small saucepan, combine jelly, catsup, vinegar and ½ teaspoon chili powder. Bring to boiling and reduce heat, simmering another 2 minutes. Brush roast with the glaze; sprinkle top with crushed corn chips. Continue roasting 10 to 15 minutes more. Remove roast from oven, let stand 10 minutes. Measure pan drippings including any corn chips adding water to make 1 cup. Heat to boiling and pass with the meat.

AVOCADO-BEAN SALAD:
Combine:

½ cup salad oil
**3 tablespoons tarragon
or wine vinegar**
3 tablespoons lemon juice
1 tablespoon sugar
1 teaspoon chili powder
¼ teaspoon salt
Dash of pepper

Pour this dressing over one 15-ounce can garbanzo beans, one 15-ounce can New Orleans Style kidney beans (Van-Camp) and 6 sliced green onions. Chill thoroughly and at serving time, spoon beans into avocados which have been halved lengthwise. This will serve eight.

ANNIVERSARY CROWN ROAST OF PORK

*Prepared for an Anniversary celebration—this filled crown roast of pork is exquisite and one of my favorites. You will be amazed at how easily this entree is accomplished. Celebration Salad, and Dar's Mud Pie adapt splendidly to Anniversary Crown Pork. Allowing two ribs per person, have your favorite (or unfavorite) butcher shape two or more sections into a **crown**. Cover ends of bones with cubes of bread or salt pork; remove these before serving. Place on rack in open roasting pan. Fill center with Kay's Bread Stuffing below. Roast according to weight—40 to 45 minutes per pound for a 6 or 7 pound roast at 325 degrees. Do not flour; add no water and do not baste during roasting—which is the method for cooking any fresh pork roast. (Before serving replace the bread or salt pork from ends of bones and top with **paper frills** which can be purchased at most kitchenware stores).*

KAY'S BREAD STUFFING:

Quantity according to use:

Cubed fresh bread
Chopped celery fairly fine
Chopped onion fairly fine
Chopped hard-boiled egg

Add salt, pepper and melted butter to taste. Just before using add one or two raw eggs according to the amount of dressing being made and then add water or chicken broth—just enough to moisten so it will cling together but not get too wet. Chopped apple, oysters, sausage, or pecans may be added if desired.

BONUS: This dressing is marvelous for stuffing that festive turkey or for any other *stuffing* utilization. You could also use it for Crown Roast of Lamb. If you prefer an alternative filling, (but once you've experienced Kay's Bread Stuffing, you won't), fill roasted Crown with mashed potatoes, mashed sweet potatoes, buttered peas and carrots, buttered cauliflower or buttered peas and mushrooms.

GRILLED BARBECUED PORK CHOPS

Provide bibs, hand out hot/steamed washcloths to your guests and serve the best Grilled Barbecued Pork Chops in town! Luau Beans as an aside will humor the chops (and friends), and Pineapple Bars will most definitely tickle the palate.

12 center cut pork chops

1—32-ounce bottle of catsup
¼ cup vegetable oil

In a flat baking pan with a lid—or other 9x13-inch covered pan, mix together the catsup and vegetable oil. Dip each pork chop in the sauce, covering both sides. Marinate for two or three hours.

When the coals are red hot, barbecue the pork chops, spooning any of the remaining sauce on the chops while grilling. Be sure to turn the pork chops over so that both sides get crunchy, gooey and messy to eat. Of course, one is encouraged to handle the pork chop bones so that the crunchy, cooked sauce can be totally enjoyed.

Yield: Plan on at least two pork chops per person.

BONUS: This recipe is so simple—you may be tempted to pass it up—DON'T—you will be missing one of the best barbecued pork chops anywhere. You can use ribs in place of the pork chops if desired.

VEGETABLE/STEAK ORIENTAL

Stir-fry advocates will enjoy this easy-to-fix combination. It is even better served with rice, tossed greens with Lora's Versatile Salad Dressing, and Meringued Rhubarb.

1 pound round steak
¼ cup corn oil

1 cup green pepper strips

1 cup diagonally sliced
  celery
1 cup sliced fresh
  mushrooms
½ cup coarsely chopped
  onion
1 can (16 ounces) bean
  sprouts, drained
1—5 ounce can water sliced
  water chestnuts (drained)
1 teaspoon salt
¼ teaspoon ginger
Several dashes pepper—
  fresh ground would be
  nicer
1½ tablespoons cornstarch
1 cup beef broth
1 tablespoon soy sauce

Cut steak diagonally across grain into thin slices, then cut into 2-inch strips. Heat corn oil in skillet over medium heat. Add meat; brown on all sides, turning as needed.
Stir in vegetables salt, ginger and pepper. Cook stirring constantly, about 3 minutes or just until tender.

Stir together cornstarch, beef broth and soy sauce until smooth. stir into vegetable/beef mixture in skillet. Bring to boil, stirring constantly and continue boiling 1 minute.

Yield: 6 generous servings.

PEKING ROAST
(commonly known as Black Beef)

An old tried and true way to cook beef. It is so aromatic that you will hardly be able to contain yourself before the cooking time is up and you can taste-test. Originated for cheaper cuts of beef, I prefer to use a top round roast, sirloin or even a nice rump roast. The Black Beef is terrific served with Baked Potatoes Holiday, Cranberry Fluff and Cheesecake Kittredge.

3—5 pound roast

Using a knife to cut slits halfway down through the meat—insert slivers of onion and garlic. Onions alone may be used if you do not care for garlic. Put the beef in a glass bowl and pour one cup of vinegar over it making sure it runs down into the slits. Cover and place in refrigerator for at least 24 hours. Make sure you make lots of slits to hide the onion and garlic.

Next day, discard the vinegar solution and place meat in a heavy roaster and brown in oil until nearly burned on both sides. (Kitchen will smell like it's burning). Pour two cups of strong black coffee over the roast. Add two cups of water and cover. Cook this slowly on simmer for six hours on top of stove. DO NOT SEASON until 20 minutes before serving, then add salt and pepper. Nothing else.

I add one-half cup whiskey to the boiling mixture, but you may omit it. However, I believe this is what makes the roast ever so tender and the alcohol will cook up and is not noticeable. And the gravy is absolutely the best ever. It may be thickened (as for any roast gravy) or left as is.

If you cook your roast too fast or if lid on the roaster is not tight, you may have to add some additional water—if so—add only one cup of water at a time.

BONUS: Peking Roast can be made ahead of time if you are expecting guests. The black meat is somewhat different and everyone will ask for the recipe—tell them it can be found in *Best of Friends, Etc.*

BONUS: Don't be afraid to almost burn the beef while browning. . .that's what makes it so delicious and the best gravy ever.

STUFFED HAMBURGERS

An unpretentious hamburger—this is not... Stuffed Hamburgers are a bit more ostentatious, but not overburdensome to create. I am certain your guests will heartily approve.

Hugh Ford's Potato Rolls, Strawberry Ring Mold, Exotic Celery and Brandy Cornucopias will be pleasant company to the Stuffed Hamburgers.

**2 pounds of lean
  ground round**
¼ cup tomato juice
¼ cup moist bread crumbs
1 egg
¼ cup red dinner wine
**1 tablespoon instant minced
  onion**
1 teaspoon salt

Mix well and divide equally into 12 parts. Flatten each into a circle.

FILLING:

**Saute 1 cup thinly sliced
  fresh mushrooms in
  3 tablespoons butter.**

Remove from heat and add:

¼ cup moist bread crumbs
1 cup shredded Swiss cheese
¾ teaspoon Fines Herbes
1 teaspoon salt

Toss filling lightly to combine. Place 1 tablespoon of filling on each of 6 patties. Fold meat mixture around filling, crimping edges together so that stuffing cannot escape.

Saute the stuffed rounds in 2 tablespoons butter until just browned, on both sides.

Add:

1½ cups tomato juice with ¼ teaspoon Fines Herbes seasoning.

Cover and simmer for ½ hour.

Blend: 2 teaspoons Arrowroot (or cornstarch) with 2 tablespoons water, stir into tomato mixture until thickened (add more tomato juice while cooking if you desire more gravy).

Yield: Serves 6

BONUS: You can double this recipe nicely if you are serving up to 12 guests. One Stuffed Hamburger is more than plentiful for one serving.

BEEF WILD RICE CASSEROLE

Extraordinarily versatile—Beef Wild Rice Casserole is readily adaptable to brunch, lunch or dinner, and served with a White Zinfandel, Marinated Combination Salad and Brandy Snap Cornucopias— creates an unsurpassable menu for dinner.

1½ - 2 pounds ground round
   (or extra lean ground beef)
¾ cup wild rice (uncooked)
1—8-ounce can mushrooms
   with juice
1 can cream of mushroom
   soup
1 can cream of celery soup
1—2 large onions chopped
¾—1 cup dry red cooking
   wine

Brown the ground round. Add chopped onion and cook with beef until transparent. Mix together the browned beef and all other ingredients in a covered casserole.
Bake in a 325 degree oven in covered casserole. Check after 2 hours— you may need to turn oven down to 300 degrees and cook another hour.

Yield: 8 to 10 servings

BONUS: You can replace the chopped onions with a package of Lipton's Onion soup. If you choose to make this substitution, add the soup to the meat in casserole.

FLAVORFUL MEATBALLS

Your guests will never guess that the exciting flavor in these bite-size meatballs is coffee. Serve the meatballs as an appeteaser or for a main course.

1 teaspoon instant coffee
¾ cup hot milk
1½ cups soft bread crumbs
¼ cup chopped onion

¼ cup butter
¼ teaspoon ground nutmeg
1½ teaspoons salt
1/8 teaspoon pepper
1 egg—slightly beaten
1 pound ground lean beef
¼ cup flour
1 cup milk

Combine 1 teaspoon instant coffee and the hot milk. Stir until coffee is dissolved. Pour over bread crumbs. Set aside. Saute the onion in butter until golden brown. Remove from heat.
Add onion to bread and coffee mixture and blend. Add nutmeg, salt, pepper and the egg—mix well. Add ground beef and mix thoroughly.
Shape into 1-inch balls and roll in the ¼ cup flour. Brown meat balls in butter remaining in skillet.
Pour milk over browned meat balls, cover and simmer 5 minutes. Remove from heat, arrange meat balls on serving dish and keep hot.

1 teaspoon instant coffee
1½ tablespoons flour
2 tablespoons water
¼ to ½ cup hot water

Stir to blend, add to milk and drippings in skillet, and blend well. Return to heat, cook and stir until smooth and thickened. Then continue to cook and stir, adding small amount of hot water gradually until gravy is of desired consistency. Season to taste with salt and pepper.
Pour the gravy over the meatballs and serve at once.

Yield: 6 main dish servings—12 appeteaser servings

SKEWERED BEEF

A special summertime treat although skewered beef can be done in the oven if you do not have access to a barbeque.

2 pounds sirloin or
   round steak (¾ inch thick)

½ cup vegetable oil
½ cup lemon juice
½ cup minced onion
1 teaspoon salt
½ teaspoon Accent
¼ teaspoon pepper
1 teaspoon Worcestershire
   sauce
1 bay leaf

2 onions quartered
2 green peppers, cut in
   1-inch cubes
18 cherry tomatoes
Fresh mushrooms
Canned potatoes

Cut meat in 1 or 2-inch chunks.

Combine the vegetable oil, lemon juice, minced onion and seasonings in a glass bowl. Add the meat chunks, cover and refrigerate overnight, turning a few times.

Alternate beef cubes, onion, green pepper and tomato on long skewers. Grill about 6-7 inches above glowing coals, turning frequently and basting with remaining marinade until beef is cooked to desired doneness—about 20 minutes.

Yield: 6 servings

BONUS: Right before removing skewers for serving, add a fresh mushroom or two and a couple of the *canned* little potatoes. Return to grill and basting once on each side, cook just until mushrooms and potatoes are heated through.

ZESTY BARBECUED RIBS

The zesty sauce on these ribs make them finger-licking good!

6 pounds pork spare ribs

Water
2 cups catsup
½ cup reconstituted lemon juice
½ cup firmly packed brown sugar
½ cup prepared mustard
½ cup finely chopped onion
¼ cup Worcestershire sauce
1 clove garlic, minced (optional)
¼ teaspoon salt
4 dashes hot pepper sauce (Tabasco)

In a large pan with lid, cook the ribs in boiling water 45-60 minutes or until tender.

Meanwhile, in medium saucepan, combine the remaining ingredients and simmer for 20 minutes, stirring occasionally.

Remove ribs to grill. Grill ribs turning and brushing frequently with the sauce. Cook until sauce *sticks to the ribs* and takes on that *finger licking* glow.

Refrigerate any leftovers.

Yield: Should feed 6 to 8 generously.

BONUS: Sauce is also great on hamburgers and chicken. Spare ribs could be accomplished in the oven if the weather doesn't agree with the barbecue—but they definitely are best if cooked on a grill.

HONOLULU SAUERBRATEN

*Honolulu Sauerbraten is a wonderful German dish either carried to the island by **tourists** or created by a Honolulu native. Whatever the derivation—this version is less complicated than most—and every bit as savory!*

2½ - 4 pounds boneless beef

2 cups red wine
2 cups beer
2 medium onions
1 clove garlic
2 bay leaves
2 ounces white vinegar
½ lemon, sliced
¼ teaspoon MSG (optional)
Salt and pepper to taste

Mix all ingredients and cover the meat. Add more beer and wine if necessary. Marinate meat for 36 to 48 hours, turning occasionally.

Brown meat in bacon fat (or vegetable oil) in very hot pan. Strain marinade, save liquid and onions.

In separate pot, brown onions in 1 tablespoon bacon fat. Add ½ teaspoon gravy coloring (Kitchen Bouquet) and add strained liquid. Add meat and pan drippings. Cover pot and bring to slow boil for about 2 hours until meat is tender.

Remove meat and strain gravy. Return liquid to pot and thicken with a mixture of cornstarch and water. Replace meat in pot and simmer for 10 minutes.

Serve with spaetzle.

LEMON SHRIMP ORIENTAL

Lemon Shrimp Oriental fits into that stir-fry **groupette** *and it includes fish, vegetables and rice. What more could you beg for— except perhaps Molded Waldorf Salad and a light serving of Espresso Charlotte—!*

1 **pound large shrimp
(fresh or frozen)—shelled
and deveined**
½ **pound fresh mushrooms,
sliced**
1 **cup celery—sliced on bias**
1 **medium green pepper—cut
in strips**
¼ **cup sliced green onion**
2 **tablespoons vegetable oil**

1—6 **ounce package frozen
pea pods**

2 **tablespoons cornstarch**
1 **teaspoon sugar**
1 **teaspoon salt**
1 **teaspoon chicken bouillon
granules**
A **few twists of the pepper
mill**
1 **cup water**
½ **teaspoon grated lemon
peel**
3 **tablespoons lemon juice**

Hot cooked rice

Cook the shelled and deveined shrimp, mushrooms, green pepper, celery and onion in hot oil 5 to 6 minutes, stirring constantly. Add pea pods. Cook and stir 1—2 minutes more. Combine the cornstarch, sugar, salt, bouillon and pepper. Blend in water, lemon peel and juice. Stir into shrimp mixture. Cook and stir until thickened and bubbly.

Serve over hot rice.

Yield: 4—6 servings

BONUS: If the shrimp are No. 52's (as they call them in the fish market)— they are large, you can count about 12 to a pound—so mull over the guest list to see if one pound will do it—if not double the recipe or whatever fits into your guest log.

SHRIMP AU GRATIN

A pleasant entree of Shrimp and sauce, baked in shells. You might find the Tomato Aspic friendly to the Shrimp Au Gratin, but per chance something is lacking, make up for it by serving Blum's Coffee Toffee Pie—it is magnificent—and guaranteed to leave your guests totally awed!

Simmer together:

5 tablespoons butter
½ teaspoon salt
¼ teaspoon freshly ground
    pepper
2 teaspoons minced onion
¼ teaspoon Worcestershire
    sauce
¼ teaspoon paprika
¾ cup mushrooms

Add:

2 teaspoons minced green
    pepper
1 teaspoon minced parsley
1 tablespoon cheese
    (cheddar, Monterey Jack,
    swiss, etc.)

Add:

2 tablespoons flour and stir
until smooth; stir in ¾ cup
milk and add 1 pound
cleaned, cooked and de-
veined shrimp.

Cook 15 minutes

Spoon into baking shells (or au gratin dishes), top with buttered bread crumbs and bake in 325 degree oven for one-half hour.

Yield: 6 servings

SEAFOOD TETRAZINNI

*An elegant **hot dish** with crabmeat and shrimp—enticing and easy on the budget. Winter Fruit Bowl, Huckleberry Muffins, and Broken Glass Torte are vital additions to Seafood Tetrazinni.*

1—8 ounce package shell macaroni
1 tablespoon butter
1—10-ounce can cream of celery soup
1—4-ounce can mushrooms stems and pieces
1 cup dairy sour cream
½ cup grated sharp cheddar cheese
2 tablespoons cooking sherry (optional)
1—6-ounce can crabmeat
1—6-ounce can shrimp

Cook the macaroni in salted water al dente; drain.
Combine soup, mushrooms, sour cream, cheese and sherry.

Dust off your nicest casserole, grease it and make three layers of the macaroni, seafood, and soup mixture in that order.

Bake at 325 degrees for 30 minutes.

Yield: 6—8

SCAMPI

Not a better Scampi anywhere! This simplistic Shrimp entree is beyond words—you will be thrilled with the finished product. Flaky croissants, a tossed salad and Trifle de Fete are more than adequate to complete this menu.

2 pounds jumbo shrimp in the shell, fresh or fresh frozen
4 tablespoons butter
2 tablespoons good, imported olive oil
2 tablespoons vegetable oil
2 tablespoons fresh parsley— snipped
4 tablespoons fresh lemon juice

Peel, devein and butterfly the shrimp, leaving the tails on.

Preheat oven to 450 degrees.

Put butter in flat baking dish, appropriate size for the shrimp. Place in preheated oven and heat until butter is foamy. Remove dish from oven.

Add the remaining ingredients to

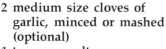

2 medium size cloves of
garlic, minced or mashed
(optional)
1 teaspoon salt
½ teaspoon dillweed
(don't leave out)
Fresh ground pepper

butter in baking dish and stir to blend.

Add shrimp, turning to coat with butter mixture. Arrange shrimp.

Bake for 6 minutes (medium shrimp) or 8—10 minutes for extra large shrimp. Turn once while cooking.

Remove from oven and serve immediately with any remaining butter mixture.

FILET OF SOLE BUNDLES

Filet of Sole Bundles is a dramatic method of serving an otherwise unimpressive piece of fish. Shrimp and mushrooms lend themselves graciously to this entree. Fresh spinach leaves splashed with Blender Caesar Dressing, Fresh Cranberry Nut Loaf and My Favorite Chocolate Cake with Filling will top off this repast delightfully.

8—10 filets of Sole
1 onion—chopped
1 cup cooked shrimp
2—4-ounce cans mushrooms
2 tablespoons butter
2—10-ounce cans mushroom
soup
¾ cup dry white wine
¾ cup shredded cheddar
cheese

Sprinkle the filets with salt, pepper and paprika.
Spread onion on each filet.
Saute the shrimp and mushrooms in butter; spread some of this mixture on each filet.
Roll and fasten each filet with toothpicks and place in a shallow baking pan.

Mix the soup and wine and pour over the Sole. Scatter the cheese over all.

Bake in 400 degree oven for 20 minutes.

Yield: 8 servings

SHRIMP AND SCALLOPS SWISS

An amiable blending of Swiss cheese and spices makes the sauce for the shrimp and scallops a pleasant experience. Resist everything but temptation and enjoy Old-fashioned Lemon Meringue Pie as an encore.

¾ **cup butter**
¾ **cup all-purpose flour**
3 **cups milk**
¾ **pound imported Swiss
cheese—shredded**
1 **small clove garlic,
minced**
1 **tablespoon salt**
¼ **teaspoon white pepper**
¼ **teaspoon dry mustard**
2 **teaspoons tomato paste**
2 **teaspoons lemon juice**

Make a cream sauce in the top of a double boiler with the butter, flour and milk. Add the cheese and stir until melted. Add the remaining ingredients and blend.

1 **pound scallops**
1 **teaspoon lemon juice**

Poach the scallops in water to which is added the lemon juice for about 10 minutes. Set aside the scallops, but add ½ cup of the broth to cream sauce.

1 **pound sliced fresh
mushrooms**
2 **tablespoons butter**

Saute the mushrooms in the butter and add them to the cream sauce.

1 **pound cooked, peeled
and deveined shrimp.**

Add the shrimp to the cream sauce above and heat to blend flavors.

Serve from chafing dish on Melba toast or in Patty Shells.

Yield: 8 generous servings

OVEN CRISPED TROUT

When you are lucky enough to have some fresh trout (or comparable species) in your refrigerator, try this mouth watering delight.

6—dressed pan-size fish
¼ cup soft butter
½ cup chopped parsley
1 egg
¼ cup milk
1 teaspoon salt
¾ cup toasted or dried bread crumbs
½ cup shredded Swiss cheese
2 tablespoons butter

Sprinkle the insides of fish with salt and pepper.

Combine the softened butter and parsley. Spread this mixture inside each fish.

Beat the egg with milk and salt. Combine bread crumbs and cheese.

Dip each fish in egg mixture and roll in crumbs.

Place fish in buttered baking pan. Dot with butter and bake in very hot oven (500 degrees) for 15 to 20 minutes or until fish is flaky and brown.

BONUS: If you have a friend who will bone the fish for you—that is when you promise him or her almost anything to handle that task for you. It is the only way to cook the fish in this recipe—I think.

POLYNESIAN FISH

Halibut takes on a new twist cooked Polynesian style. A fresh fruit bowl with Best Fruit Dressing is my choice for accompanying the halibut together with a basket of Dixie's Sky High Biscuits and strawberry jam. Mocha Alaska Pie is a befitting dessert.

3 pounds halibut—
cut into *steaks*
⅓ cup lime juice
¼ cup melted butter
½ teaspoon salt
¼ teaspoon freshly ground
pepper
Generous pinch of marjoram

½ can (10 ounce) cream of
shrimp soup
½ cup commercial
sour cream
3—4 green onions with tops,
thinly sliced
½ cup tiny shrimp

Wash, dry and cut fish into 6 serving pieces. Place in oven-proof shallow dish. Pour lime juice over top and allow to soak for a few minutes on each side. Pour melted butter over fish and sprinkle with seasonings. Broil 10 minutes. Baste once with the butter. Remove from heat, baste again with oven juices. Set aside and cool.

Mix the soup and sour cream together. Spoon on top of fish. Bake 30 minutes at 325 degrees.

Before serving, garnish with the tiny shrimp and sliced green onions.

CREAMY MEXICAN CHICKEN ENCHILADAS

Another delectable variation of the Mexican enchilada. Flour tortillas encase a spicy chicken filling topped with sour cream and cheese. A tossed green salad splashed with Lora's Versatile Salad Dressing and English Toffee Bars create a winning combination.

**12 flour tortillas,
room temperature**

¹/₂ cup chopped onion
**1—4-ounce can mushrooms,
stems and pieces, drained**
1 clove garlic, minced
2 tablespoons butter
**2 cups finely chopped
cooked chicken—
chicken breasts are best**
**1—4-ounce can chopped
green chilies—drained**
1 cup dairy sour cream
1¹/₂ teaspoons chili powder
1 teaspoon ground cumin
¹/₂ teaspoon salt
¹/₄ teaspoon pepper
**4 cups shredded cheddar
cheese**

Cooking oil
**4 cups shredded cheddar
cheese**
2 cups dairy sour cream

In large skillet, saute the onion and garlic until tender. Add the mushrooms, chicken, chilies, 1 cup sour cream, chili powder, cumin, salt and pepper. Heat over low heat, stirring frequently until hot. Remove from heat.

Pour oil into small (8 inch) skillet, filling about ¹/₂ inch deep. Dip tortillas one at a time into oil and fry several seconds until they begin to blister and become limp. DO NOT LET THEM BECOME CRISP. Remove with tongs and drain on paper toweling.

Spread a generous tablespoon of filling down center of each tortilla. Sprinkle with cheese, fold sides over filling and place seam down in a greased 9x13-inch baking dish. Repeat with remaining tortillas.

Bake in 350 degree oven for 15 minutes. Remove from oven and spread with the 2 cups sour cream and scatter any remaining cheddar cheese over top. Bake 8 minutes more, WATCHING CAREFULLY that sour cream does not curdle.

BONUS: An eye-opening Margarita would be a great beginning to this entree.

BEEF ENCHILADAS

Unlike Creamy Chicken Enchiladas, the beef variation has its own sauce, specially prepared by the cook. These enchiladas also request corn tortillas.

1 pound lean ground beef
12 corn tortillas

3 tablespoons flour
2—14 ounce cans tomato
   sauce
½ teaspoon pepper
2 tablespoons chili powder
1 teaspoon Worcestershire

1 white peeled onion—
   chopped
3—4 cups shredded sharp
   cheddar cheese

In a large skillet or electric frypan, brown the ground beef. Remove from skillet with slotted spoon and set aside.

To the pan drippings, add the flour, stirring to scrape loose any of the browned beef crumblies, and add the tomato sauce together with all of the seasonings. Simmer on low heat 15—20 minutes. If sauce becomes too thick, add a little water to thin down.

Meanwhile—pour cooking oil into an 8-inch skillet, filling it about ½ inch deep. Fry corn tortillas until soft, drain each on paper towels and stack for filling. Remove sauce from heat and with tongs slide a cooked tortilla through the sauce, place on a plate and spoon a heaping tablespoon of the browned beef and some of the raw onion and cheese down center of tortilla. Roll up and secure with toothpicks if necessary. Continue with this procedure, laying Enchiladas side by side in two 9x13-inch baking dishes. When all tortillas have been filled, pour remaining sauce on top, sprinkle with any remaining onion and cheese and bake in 350 degree oven 15—20 minutes.

BONUS: I usually freeze a portion of the recipe if I am not planning to have guests for dinner. If you wish to freeze, hold off putting sauce on top. Store remaining sauce in a container and freeze. Remove enchiladas from freezer and bring to room temperature. Heat the sauce and pour over top of enchiladas before baking. You can add the onions and cheese on top before freezing.

FREEZER BURRITOS BELLINGHAM

A super, spicy beef and cheese burrito. Terrifically uncomplicated and satisfying enough to please the heartiest appetites.

3 pounds lean ground beef
1—4-ounce can chopped
  green chilies
2—7-ounce bottles taco
  salsa sauce
1 bunch green onions—
  tops and all—chopped
1 can chopped ripe olives

24 flour tortillas
1—16-ounce can refried beans
2 pounds Monterey Jack
  cheese
2 cups dairy sour cream

Brown and drain ground beef (can be done under broiler). Mix together with chilies, taco sauce, green onions and olives.

Spread each tortilla with refried beans, spoon meat mixture down center, sprinkle shredded cheese on top of meat, and roll up envelope style. Place in baking dish, top with more Jack cheese and sour cream.

Bake 30—45 minutes at 350 degrees.

BONUS: Great for a big party—but if you don't need 24 burritos all at once, freeze what you don't need—without the sour cream.

CHIMICHANGAS

Sounds like something that belongs on a dance floor. However, these spicy filled tortillas are a taco variation neatly wrapped in a bundle-like flour tortilla, and deep fried until flaky. Try them soon, they are flavorful, different, fun to make and economically sound.

1 pound lean ground beef
1 medium white peeled
  onion, chopped
  (about ½ cup)
1—8¼ ounce can refried
  beans with green chilies
1 tomato, peeled, seeded
  and chopped
1½ teaspoons dried minced
  parsley
2 tablespoons salsa
1½ teaspoons oregano
¾ teaspoon cumin
1½ cups chopped or
  sliced ripe olives

8 flour tortillas
Vegetable oil for frying
Grated Monterey Jack or
  cheddar cheese
Shredded lettuce
Cherry tomatoes, halved
Dairy sour cream

Cook the beef and onion in skillet until beef is browned—about five minutes. Remove from heat. Mix in the beans, tomato, parsley, salsa, oregano, cumin and one-half of the olives.

Fry each tortilla in oiled skillet until it just begins to get crisp. Drain and quickly spoon filling down center. Fold in sides and then roll up around filling. Secure with toothpick.

Heat one to one and a half inches vegetable oil in deepsided skillet. Fry two or three rolls at a time—depending on size of pan—turn once, until golden. This should take about 2 to 3 minutes. Remove from oil, drain on paper toweling and remove picks. Keep warm while completing procedure with remaining Chimichangas.

Serve with bowls of remaining olives, cheese, lettuce, tomatoes and sour cream as desired.

BONUS: For a large party, you may want to prepare and fry the Chimichangas ahead. Reheat in oven just before serving.

JOSE'S DELIGHT

Terrific served with a frosty glass of Mexican beer—but also good without the beer. Tortilla Bread is a great fill-in.

1 pound lean ground beef
1 large white peeled onion, chopped
1—4-ounce can green chilies
1—8-ounce can tomato sauce
1 cup canned tomatoes
1—15-ounce can Van Camps New Orleans Style red kidney beans
¼ teaspoon oregano
2 tablespoons chili powder
¼ teaspoon cumin
1—10 ounce bag regular-size corn chips
1 cup grated Monterey Jack cheese
Chopped lettuce
Chopped onion

In a bit of cooking oil, saute onion and ground beef together. Stir in the green chilies, tomato sauce, tomatoes, and seasonings. Dig out your best casserole, butter it and alternate the beef layer, beans, corn chips, and cheese. Repeat the layers ending with corn chips and cheese.

Bake it, covered, in 350 degree oven for 35 minutes.

Take off lid and bake for another 10 minutes.

Just before serving, scatter some crisp chopped lettuce and onion on top of Jose's Delight.

Yield: 6 servings

BURNHAM'S BLOOMSDAY SPAGHETTI SAUCE

*Reputed to be the best **carbo-feed** in the northwest is Kent Burnham's Bloomsday Spaghetti Sauce. For those fortunate few who participated in Kent's 1986 pre-Bloomsday Run carbo-feed . . here is his famous Bloomsday Spaghetti Sauce, to-wit:*

4 pounds lean ground beef
4 quarts home-canned
   tomatoes (or 4—32 ounce
   cans commercially canned
   tomatoes)
1 cup finely chopped onion
1—3-ounce can mushrooms
3—3-ounce packages
   commercial spaghetti
   sauce mix (Lawry's, etc.)
½ cup *cheap* red wine
1 teaspoon curry powder
1 teaspoon minced garlic
½ teaspoon sage
¼ teaspoon ground pepper
Salt to taste

Brown the beef, onion, curry powder, garlic, sage, salt and pepper in a large skillet. Drain off any grease.

Add the *cheap* wine. Cover and simmer for five minutes.

In a large stock pot, heat the tomatoes; add the beef mixture. When the beef et al is heated through, add mushrooms and commercial spaghetti sauce mix.

Simmer on low heat for as long as you have time to be in the kitchen (or at least in the area)—two to three hours is best.

Yield: Five quarts of delicious thick sauce.

BONUS: Kent says the sauce is in its prime when made a few days before serving, frozen and reheated.

SPAGHETTI SAUCE WITH DISTINCTION

An assertive spaghetti sauce with substance, and frees the chef for preparing Macadamia Nut Creme Rum Pie as a grand finale to a splendiforous spaghetti dinner, and Alpha-Dough-Me's that replace the worn-out breadstick accomplice.

1 pound round steak,
(¼-inch thick)
cut into cubes
2 pounds lean ground beef
2 teaspoons vegetable oil
2 garlic cloves, minced
(optional)
5 stalks celery,
thinly sliced, with some
of the leaves
2 white onions, chopped
1 green pepper, chopped
30 ounces tomato paste
2 - 16-ounce cans
whole tomatoes
1 - 15-ounce can
tomato sauce
1½ cups dry red wine
1 small bunch parsley,
chopped
2 tablespoons dried
basil flakes
1 tablespoon oregano
1 tablespoon marjoram
2 teaspoons thyme
½ teaspoon rosemary
6 whole black peppercorns
4 dried chile peppers
crushed or 1 teaspoon
chile pepper flakes
2 - 4-ounce cans mushroom
stems and pieces

Brown the steak cubes and ground beef together in the vegetable oil in large skillet. Remove and hold aside. In the same pan, saute the garlic and onions until golden. Remove and hold aside. Then cook pepper and celery until tender. In a large stock pot add the cooked ingredients together with the tomato paste, whole tomatoes with liquid, wine, mushrooms, parsley and all seasonings. Cover the pan and simmer 3 hours, stirring occasionally to keep the sauce from sticking.

Serve with spaghetti, cooked *al dente*.

BONUS: This recipe makes 4 over-sized quarts. It is best reheated the next day and even better after frozen—the seasoning becomes more intense. There is enough sauce to serve a very large group. It is also great to put to use as the Meat Sauce for Rigatoni—with lots of freshly ground parmesan cheese.

BETTY'S FAVORITE LASAGNE

*I call this Betty's Favorite because I gave this recipe to her several years ago—I will stake my life on it—she has some in her freezer now...that's how **favorite** it is to her.*

1 box of lasagne noodles, drain and *hold* in cold water until the following sauce is ready:

**Saute
2 tablespoons minced onion in 2 tablespoons olive oil or vegetable oil for 3—5 minutes—do not burn**

**ADD:
1½ pounds lean hamburger —cook 10 minutes or until browned.**

**ADD:
2—8 ounce cans tomato sauce
1 cup beef boullion (1 cube to 1 cup water— don't leave out)
¼ teaspoon pepper
1½ teaspoon salt
½ teaspoon each— basil and oregano
¼ teaspoon crushed dried red pepper flakes (this is optional, but if you like a little *oomph* in your sauce—this is excellent)**

Simmer the sauce 30 minutes.

Spoon some of the sauce in a greased 9 x 13 baking dish or other rectangular casserole—THEN LAYER AS FOLLOWS:

LASAGNE NOODLES
SAUCE
GRATED MOZZARELLA CHEESE
REPEAT LAYERS UNTIL SAUCE
   IS ALL USED.
END WITH CHEESE LAYER

BAKE uncovered at 375 degrees for 20 to 30 minutes.

BONUS: This freezes very well— without baking first. Just put it together, cover well with foil or plastic wrap and freeze. Thaw before baking.

I sometimes use a combination of Monterey Jack Cheese, Mozzarella and Parmesan on the top layer—gives it a little more pizazz.

You can double this recipe—use one for dinner—and freeze the other for one of those days when *surprise* guests arrive in time for dinner.

PASTICCIO

*A most flavorful one-dish entree with familiar Greek spices. Pasticcio is **easy** to prepare and even **easier** to consume. Canlis' Special Salad is particularly refreshing with Pasticcio. A big slice of Fresh Apple Cake will leave your guests in a most satisfying frame of mind.*

1½ cups pasticcio macaroni (Mezzani)
1 beaten egg
¼ cup milk
⅓ cup grated parmesan cheese
¾ pound lean ground beef
½ cup chopped onion
1 8-ounce can tomato sauce
½ teaspoon ground cinnamon
1/8 teaspoon ground nutmeg
¾ teaspoon salt
1/8 teaspoon pepper

3 tablespoons butter or margarine
3 tablespoons all-purpose flour
¼ teaspoon salt
1½ cups milk
1 beaten egg
¼ cup grated parmesan cheese

Cook macaroni according to directions; drain.
Stir in the one beaten egg, ¼ cup milk and ⅓ cup parmesan. Set aside.

In skillet, cook the ground beef and onion until meat is lightly browned and onion is tender. Drain off excess fat. Stir in tomato sauce, cinnamon, nutmeg, ¾ teaspoon salt and pepper; set aside.
In saucepan, melt butter or margarine. Blend in flour and remaining ¼ teaspoon salt. Stir in remaining milk. Cook, stirring constantly until mixture thickens and bubbles. Cook and stir 1 minute more. Blend a moderate amount of hot mixture into remaining egg; return to saucepan. Stir in remaining cheese.
Layer half of the macaroni mixture in an 8x8x2-inch baking pan. Spoon meat mixture on top, then remaining macaroni. Spread cream sauce over macaroni.

Bake in 350 degree oven for 45 to 50 minutes. Let stand 10 minutes before serving.

Yield 6—8 servings

BONUS: Mostaccioli 84 by Ronzoni Macaroni Products can be used for the macaroni in this recipe.

VEGETABLES & SIDE DISHES:

VEGETABLES & SIDE DISHES:

PHYLLO SPINACH PIE

Served with brunch, or as a vegetable side dish to an entree, this Greek style Spinach Pie is super.

½ cup sliced green onion
½ teaspoon dried dillweed
1 tablespoon vegetable oil
1—10-ounce package frozen
   chopped spinach, thawed
4 tablespoons butter
¼ cup all-purpose flour
½ teaspoon salt
1½ cups milk
2 beaten eggs
1 cup cream-style, small curd
   cottage cheese
½ cup crumbled feta cheese
¼ teaspoon baking powder
2 16x16-inch sheets phyllo
   (filo) dough
2 tablespoons melted butter

In a skillet, cook the onion and dill in hot oil till onion is tender. Squeeze excess water from spinach; add to onion and dill. Cook until hot—keep warm. In large saucepan melt the 4 tablespoons butter and blend in flour and salt, add milk all at once. Cook and stir till mixture thickens and bubbles. Cook and stir 1 minute longer.

Add a small amount of hot mixture to the eggs; return to saucepan. Stir in cheeses, spinach mixture and baking powder.

Brush half of 1 sheet phyllo dough with some of the butter; fold in half and butter half of dough rectangle and fold again, forming an 8x8-inch square. Place in greased 8x8x2-inch baking pan, pour in spinach mixture.

Repeat folding and brushing with butter the second sheet of phyllo dough. Place this atop the spinach mixture and tuck in the edges.

Bake in 325 degree oven for 30—40 minutes, till mixture is set and top is golden. Let stand 10 minutes before cutting and serving.

Yield: 8—10 servings

WILD RICE PORTUGAISE

Another one of those nutty textured wild rice casseroles that will add flavorful excitement to a dull day-after-day routine.

1 cup wild rice—
soak overnight in cold
water, drain, rewash and
redrain.
1 cup grated Swiss cheese
1 cup fresh mushrooms,
chopped
1 cup chopped ripe black
olives
½ cup diced onion
1 cup drained, canned
diced tomatoes
½ cup salad oil
½ teaspoon salt
1 clove garlic—mashed or
minced (optional)

Combine all ingredients. Stir to mix well.

Place in buttered two quart casserole with a lid.

Bake for 1 hour at 350 degrees.

Yield: 6 servings

BONUS: Prepare early in the day, refrigerate—bake prior to dinner. I have on numerous occasions soaked the wild rice early in the A.M. before assembling later in the day.

BAKED POTATOES HOLIDAY

*A **glamorous** idea for that festive dinner and nutritious as well.*

8 baking potatoes
½ cup hot milk
¼ cup butter
1½ teaspoons salt
1/8 teaspoon pepper
1 cup shredded zucchini
(2 small)
2 tablespoons grated onion
(or 1 tablespoon dried
flakes)
¼ cup butter
1—2 ounce jar chopped
pimientos, drained

Scrub the potatoes, prick each with a fork and bake in 450 degree oven until done—approximately 45 minutes. Cut a slice from top of each potato immediately and scoop out pulp, being careful not to break the skins. Add the hot milk, ¼ cup butter, salt and pepper to hot potato pulp and mash until light and fluffy. (I do this with mixer).

Cook the zucchini and onion in ¼ cup butter for two to three minutes. Fold zucchini, onion and pimiento into the potato mixture. Spoon mixture into reserved potato shells.

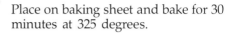

Place on baking sheet and bake for 30 minutes at 325 degrees.

Yield: 8 servings

BONUS: If potatoes are large, instead of using a whole potato per serving, slice the potato in half, scoop out the pulp and carry on with the instructions. Instead of 8 servings—you will have 16. I prefer to serve the potatoes in this fashion. You can make them in advance and reheat—increasing the time to 45 minutes.

CREAMY POTATO PUFF

Here's a unique way of serving mashed potatoes when you don't have a gravy to drizzle over them.

4 cups mashed potatoes (hot or cold)
1 8—ounce package cream cheese (softened)
1 egg—beaten
⅓ cup finely chopped onion
2 tablespoons flour
½ cup shredded carrots (optional)
¼ cup chopped pimento (optional)
1 teaspoon salt
Pepper—shake or two

Put potatoes in large bowl of your electric mixer; add cream cheese, egg, chopped onion and flour.
Mix at medium speed until well blended; then on high speed until light and fluffy. Fold in the carrots and pimento; add salt and pepper.

Spoon into a greased one-quart casserole and bake uncovered in a 300 degree oven for 35—40 minutes.

Yield: 8 servings

BONUS: You can prepare ahead and refrigerate. Best to bring to room temperature before baking.

WEDGED BAKED POTATOES

Potatoes are a nutritious part of any meal and fixed in parmesan-laced wedges portray an interesting version.

4 large baking potatoes—
  do not peel
¼ cup vegetable oil
3 tablespoons parmesan
  cheese
1 teaspoon salt
1 teaspoon paprika
½ teaspoon pepper
1/8 teaspoon garlic salt

Wash and scrub potatoes; cut in wedges. Place the wedges, skin side down in baking dish.

Mix the vegetable oil and remaining seasonings together, brush on potatoes evenly and bake in 350 degree oven for 1 hour.

BONUS: During baking period—sprinkle on more parmesan cheese for additional flavor.

CREAMED POTATO CASSEROLE

This is one of those side dishes that is very easy to prepare with the assistance of the frozen food section of your local food store. . . and tastes as though you put considerable thought and effort into it.

1 large bag frozen hash
  brown potatoes (2 pounds)
½ cup butter
1 teaspoon salt
½ teaspoon pepper
½ cup chopped onion
2 cups grated sharp Cheddar
  cheese
1—10½ ounce can Cream of
  Chicken soup
1 pint sour cream

TOPPING:

¼ cup melted butter
2 cups crushed cornflakes

Thaw potatoes and assemble in large casserole—9 x 13.

Combine the soup, ½ cup melted butter, salt, pepper, onion, cheese, and sour cream—pour over potatoes in casserole.

Spread topping over potatoes and bake at 350 degrees for 45 minutes—uncovered.

Yield: Serves 12 to 14 generously

ORANGE SWEET POTATOES

Sweet potatoes are sometimes saved for a Thanksgiving celebration. Orange Sweet Potatoes served any time of the year are in themselves festive and a refreshing treat for everyone.

6 medium size sweet
  potatoes
1 cup orange juice
2 teaspoons grated
  orange rind
1 tablespoon cornstarch
5 tablespoons melted butter
½ cup brown sugar,
  firmly packed
⅓ cup granulated sugar

Cook the potatoes in their jackets until tender.

Remove skins.

Meanwhile, combine remaining ingredients in a medium saucepan. Cook stirring until thickened.

Arrange potatoes sliced in half lengthwise in baking dish. Pour orange sauce over them, cover and bake in a 350 degree oven for 20 minutes. Uncover and bake 15 minutes longer.

Yield: 6 servings

WILD RICE CASSEROLE

*Wild rice adds elegance to any meal—and is easy to prepare. Whenever I get hung up on what to serve as a **side dish** - wild rice is my **wild card**.*

1 cup wild rice, uncooked
1 chopped white onion
3 stalks chopped celery
   (with some leaves)
1 teaspoon seasoned salt
½ cup dry white wine
2 tablespoons butter
4 cups chicken broth
   (homemade or canned)
Pepper to taste

Dig out that casserole and dust off the lid. Combine all ingredients, place in the casserole, bake covered at 325 degrees for 2 hours. Could anything be easier?

Serves 8

BONUS: Add small can of mushrooms—pieces and stems. This dish may be prepared in advance—and freezes beautifully!

WILD RICE & CASHEWS

A crunchy blend of wild rice and cashews makes this side dish an excellent choice with any entree of your choosing. I like to serve it with Palm Springs Chicken.

2 cups wild rice
2 cups sliced fresh
   mushrooms
⅓ cup butter
½ cup cashew pieces
Chopped parsley

Wash the rice thoroughly and place in large sauce pan. Cover with cold water and bring to a boil over medium heat. Drain. Repeat this procedure three times. In the last *repeat*, add salt to taste (about 1 teaspoon) and cook until tender.

Drain well.

Saute the mushrooms in butter; pour over the rice, add cashews, toss and after spooning into serving dish, sprinkle with parsley.

Yield: 8—10 generous servings.

BONUS: The ingredients can be halved if you don't need 10 servings. Also, you can make this ahead of time and reheat.

BESSIE'S BEANS

A must in everyone's **bag of tricks**. *Captivatingly simple in construction, this charming little side-dish will glean rants and raves from those who partake—men seem to be particularly enchanted with Bessie's Beans.*

3—15-ounce cans Van Camp's
  New Orleans Style
  kidney beans
6 slices lean thick-cut bacon,
  cut in half inch pieces
1 medium white peeled
  onion, chopped
Salt and pepper to taste

In a large skillet, brown the bacon. Add the chopped onion and saute for about 5 minutes. Add the three cans of beans and simmer for about 30 minutes until the bacon and onions have a chance to blend in with the beans. Salt and pepper to taste.

Yield: 10 servings

BONUS: After putting the bean dish together, you can put in a covered casserole and bake on low heat for an hour or so at 300 degrees. The beans are even better reheated the next day.

VEGETABLE MELANGE

*Definitely not superfluous—Vegetable Melange rates a gold star and deserves **top priority** as my personal choice in the vegetable/side dish category.*

1 cup slivered almonds
½ pound bacon, cut into
 one-inch strips
1 pound zucchini sliced
 in ¼ inch slices
1 pound egg plant,
 cut into one-inch cubes
1 large white onion—
 cut in wedges
¼ cup fresh parsley
1 tablespoon flour
2 cups diced fresh tomatoes
 (fill up two cup measuring
 cup to heaping)

Saute the bacon pieces in large skillet until it crisps. Remove with slotted spoon—reserve.

Saute almonds in same pan with the bacon drippings—until they are lightly browned. Remove from pan with slotted spoon, leaving drippings in pan.

Add zucchini, eggplant and onion to same pan. Add a little vegetable oil if not enough bacon fat remaining. Cover and cook over medium low heat for 15 minutes. Shake the pan or *move*

LUAU BEANS

These beans would definitely be a hit at anybody's Luau—but are adaptable to any menu requiring that basic home-style touch. Go Luau! Delectable are they.

1 medium green pepper,
 cut in 1 inch squares
¼ cup diagonally sliced
 green onions
1 clove garlic, minced
2 tablespoons butter
3½ cups Pork and Beans
½ cup pineapple tidbits
¼ cup sliced water chestnuts
1 teaspoon Soy sauce
¼ cup Molasses

Cook the pepper, onion, and garlic in butter until soft. Add remainder ingredients. Heat and serve.

Yield: 6—8 servings

BONUS: Put all ingredients (raw) in a casserole and bake at 325 degrees for 1—2 hours. I prefer this method—the flavor has a chance to *catch hold*. You can double this recipe for that ravenous crowd.

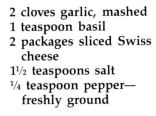

2 cloves garlic, mashed
1 teaspoon basil
2 packages sliced Swiss
 cheese
1½ teaspoons salt
¼ teaspoon pepper—
 freshly ground

vegetables to keep from sticking to pan. Remove from heat. Stir in the flour, add tomatoes and stir in parsley. Add garlic, basil, salt and pepper.

Lightly butter a two quart flat baking dish. Layer one-half of vegetable mixture in dish. Sprinkle less than half of the almonds and bacon on top of this. Top with layer of Swiss cheese, layer rest of vegetable mixture on top, then almonds and bacon, leaving some almonds and bacon unused. This amount should be much less than what was used in layering. Lastly—singly layer Swiss cheese on top and sprinkle remaining almonds and bacon over the cheese. (You will probably have a couple of slices of cheese left over).

Bake uncovered in preheated 400 degree oven 15 or 20 minutes until heated through.

Yield: 8 servings

BONUS: To serve later, cover with foil and refrigerate. One-half hour before serving take out of refrigerator—then bake at 400 degrees for 30 to 35 minutes. Should be bubbly.

BROCCOLI WITH CHEESE

The marriage of cheese and onion rings with the broccoli is definitely divine.

3 packages frozen broccoli
spears (parboiled or
microwaved for
4—5 minutes)
2—10½ cans Cream of
Mushroom soup
1—10½ ounce can evaporated
milk
1 can—Durkees French Fried
Onion Rings
2 cups shredded Cheddar
cheese

Cook and drain broccoli and separate spears into serving pieces. Place half of the broccoli spears in bottom of large, greased casserole.

Combine the two cans of soup with the evaporated milk, salt and pepper to taste and the can of french fried onion rings.

Pour half of the soup mixture over the broccoli; then place remaining broccoli spears on top of the soup and cover with remaining soup mixture. Handily sprinkle the cheese on top of layered broccoli and bake one hour at 325 degrees.

Yield: 8—10 servings

BONUS: Green beans may be substituted for the broccoli. The recipe lends well to feeding a large assembly—it can be doubled or tripled!

ALSO, if you should choose to bake longer than the 1 hour allowed, lower oven temperature to 300 degrees, sprinkle on another can of onion rings covering the cheese layer and bake another 20 minutes.

SCALLOPED CABBAGE

Don't crinkle your nose at this one! Those who usually do not like their veggies consider this dish supreme—trust me—I've watched them uncertainly taste, consume and request another serving.

4 cups cooked shredded cabbage
White sauce (your favorite will do, but see below if you don't have one)
¾ cup shredded sharp Cheddar cheese
Buttered bread crumbs

Cook the cabbage in boiling water to cover—7—8 minutes Combine with enough of the white sauce to which you have added the shredded cheese and spoon into a baking dish. Top with the buttered bread crumbs and bake in a 350 degree oven for 20 minutes.

WHITE SAUCE:

¼ cup butter
¼ cup all-purpose flour
2 cups milk
Salt & pepper to taste
One *grate* of nutmeg (fresh grated) (optional)

In saucepan, melt the butter and whisk or stir in flour until well blended and bubbly—remove from heat and gradually stir in the milk. Put back on burner and at medium heat cook, stirring constantly, until mixture thickens smoothly. Remove from heat and add seasonings. Makes 2 cups.

(If you have a double-boiler—put it to use—you'll lessen the risk of *lumping*).

CRUMB BUTTER TOPPING:

1 cup fine dry bread crumbs
¼ cup melted butter.

Mix crumbs with melted butter

Yield: 6 servings

FESTIVE CORN BAKE

*Festive befits serving this dish with hot or cold turkey slices during the holidays. It, however, lends itself well to year-around service with its **nutty** texture.*

2 cups cream-style corn
(1—1 pound-size can)
1 cup cooked, diced carrots
¼ cup finely chopped
onions (green onions are
good)
¼ cup sliced, drained ripe
olives
2 beaten eggs
1 teaspoon salt
Pepper to taste
A drop or two—Tabasco

1¾ cups soft bread crumbs
(about 3 slices bread)
1 tablespoon melted butter

Combine the corn, carrots, onion and olives. Add the eggs, salt, pepper, Tabasco and one cup of the bread crumbs. Pour into a greased 1-quart casserole. Toss the remaining ¾ cup bread crumbs with melted butter and strew atop the corn mixture. Bake in 350 degree oven, uncovered for 50 minutes. Let stand 5 minutes before serving.

Yield: 6 servings.

OVEN RATATOUILLE

Beyond the rich succulence and relatively low caloric content lies a multitude of other qualities in Ratatouille. It actually tastes better a day or two after its origination and some prefer it cold to hot!

3 large white onions, sliced
2 cloves of garlic, minced
   or mashed
2 medium eggplants, cut in
   ½ inch cubes
8 medium zucchini, thick
   sliced (don't peel)
3 green bell peppers, seeded
   and cut in chunks (1 red
   bell pepper adds variety—
   if available)
2 teaspoons salt
2 teaspoons basil leaves
½ cup minced parsley
6 large firm, ripe tomatoes
   (cut in *wedges*)

4 tablespoons good,
   imported olive oil
Mozzarella cheese

Into a 6 quart casserole layer all ingredients — onions through tomatoes— in no particular order. *Scoosh* down to make all of the veggies fit, if necessary. Drizzle the olive oil evenly over the top layer.
Cover the casserole and bake at 350 degrees for two hours.
Check periodically and baste with some of its own liquid.
During the second hour of baking, uncover and if Ratatouille is quite liquid, bake with the lid off.

Before serving—cover the Ratatouille with very thin slices of Mozzarella, place back in oven—watch carefully and serve as soon as the cheese melts (as it would do on pizza).

Yield: Serves 8—10 comfortably.

BONUS: The addition of the cheese is my own thought. I don't believe Ratatouille traditionally has the cheese layer—but it enhances an already succulent dish. You certainly may omit the cheese, but my friends assure me that it *makes* the Ratatouille.

FRESH MUSHROOMS A LA CHEESE

A deceivingly flavorful side dish that is super with a charcoaled steak and crispy green salad. The ingredients do not impress one as being anything out of the ordinary, but the finished product is worthy of guests and is destined to become a favorite.

1 pound fresh mushrooms, (get the nice big, white ones), sliced lengthwise
1 cup shredded sharp Cheddar cheese
1 8-ounce can sliced, drained black olives
1½ teaspoons flour
½ teaspoon salt
Pepper—a couple grinds on the pepper mill
⅓ cup Half-and-Half cream
1½ tablespoons butter
1 cup fresh bread crumbs

In a buttered 2-quart casserole, (I use a large quiche dish) arrange the mushrooms, cheese and olives — alternating layers. Blend together the flour, salt, pepper and half-and-half and pour over the mushrooms.

Melt the butter in a small sauce pan, add the fresh bread crumbs and mix with a fork. Sprinkle the crumbs over the mushroom mixture and bake uncovered in a 350 degree oven for about 30 minutes.

Yield: 8 servings

BONUS: This can be made up a few hours ahead of time and held hostage (covered with plastic wrap) in the refrigerator until ready to bake.

VEGETABLE STRATA

*A perfect **crowd-pleaser** to add to that special buffet celebration.*

2 cups canned green beans
(drained)
2 cups celery—biasly sliced
2 cups carrots, sliced
1 large onion sliced
4 tomatoes—cut in wedges
1 green or red bell pepper,
sliced
1—8 ounce can water
chestnuts—drained
¼ cup butter (one-half of
one stick)

DRY MIX:
1½ tablespoons tapioca
¾ teaspoon seasoned salt
1 tablespoon sugar
1 teaspoon salt
½ teaspoon pepper

In a 1 quart casserole layer one-half of the above vegetables. Sprinkle with the DRY MIX.

Layer with the remaining vegetables, dot with ¼ cup butter.

Bake covered in 350 degree oven for 1 hour; uncover and bake 20 minutes.

Yield: Serves 6—8

BONUS: Can be made ahead, baked and carried to the *celebration* for reheating if necessary.

Fresh green beans can replace the canned version and are a great replacement.

EXOTIC CELERY

*Celery somehow is regarded as a **plain Jane** item and an edible that belongs in casseroles, soups and salads. Exotic Celery will be a pleasant surprise for those who have previously strewn it about unassumingly!*

4 cups celery (sliced on bias)

Boil for 8 minutes in salted water (don't let it get mushy)

DRAIN AND ADD:

1—10-1/2 ounce can Cream of Chicken soup (undiluted)
1—8 ounce can sliced water chestnuts—drained
1—2 ounce jar chopped pimento with juice
Salt to taste
Slivered almonds

Place the combination in a casserole and bake at 350 degrees for 30 minutes. Before serving scatter slivered almonds on top of the celery for that *finished* look.

Yield: 4 servings

BONUS: Recipe doubles nicely. It can be prepared well in advance of serving—just cover and refrigerate—then bake.

DESSERTS:

Apple Crisp Grant - 210
Apricot Jam Strudel - 216
Banana Cream Pie - 198
Blarney Stones - 229
Blum's Coffee Toffee Pie - 206
Brandy Snap Cornucopias - 230
Broken Glass Torte - 217
Butter Sugar Cookies - 237
Cheesecake Kittredge - 208
Chocolate Banana Loaf - 218
Chocolate Roll - 220
Chocolate Sheet Cake - 221
Chocolate Steam Pudding - 219
Dar's Mud Pie - 201
Double Decadence Muffins - 211
English Toffee Bars - 231
Espresso Charlotte - 212
Fresh Apple Cake - 224
Fresh Huckleberry Pie - 197
Fresh Strawberry Pie - 194
Fudge Sundae Pie - 203
Gen's Baked Chocolate Pudding - 215
Gram Grady's Date Pin Wheels - 234
Harvey Wallbanger Cake - 227
Homemade Ladyfingers - 238
Huckleberry Walnut Cream Cake - 226
Kona Coffee Mocha Puffs - 228
Macadamia Nut Creme Rum Pie - 200
Meringued Rhubarb - 209
Mocha Alaska Pie - 205
My Favorite Chocolate Cake (with filling) - 222
Oatmeal Crunchies - 235
Old-fashioned Lemon Meringue Pie - 204
Orange-Slice Date Bars - 232
Peg's Peanut Butter Bars - 233
Pie Crust Supreme - 193
Pineapple Bars - 233
Rembrandt's Rhubarb Cobbler Crisp - 4
Rhubarb a la Crunch - 210
Rhubarb Cake Mary - 213
Rhubarb Surprise Pie - 199
Sacked Apple Pie - 196
Sally's Almond Lace Wafers - 239
Salted Nut Roll Squares - 240
Sour Cream Apple Pie - 195
Spicy Huckleberry Cake - 225
Strawberry Cheesecake Pie - 207
Trifle De Fete - 214
Unsurpassable Chocolate Chip Cookies - 236
Valentine's Day Pie - 199
Zucchini Chocolate Cake - 222

PIE CRUST SUPREME

*Pie Crust Supreme is the best pie crust not only for its flakiness but for its ease in creating and its versatility. I guarantee that once you try it you will never use a **ready-made** again. I dedicate this to my friends, Bev and Gootch . . .*

3 cups all-purpose flour
1 teaspoon salt
1¼ cups shortening
**   (Crisco is my choice)**
1 egg beaten
1 tablespoon cider vinegar
5 tablespoons cold water

Cut the above together (using a fork or pastry blender) until it resembles small pebbles.

Beat together until blended and pour over *pebble* mixture. Mix until blended and press into ball.

Separate into three pieces, wrap in plastic wrap and chill—for about an hour.

When you are ready to prepare the dough for pies, take one piece of dough and roll out between two sheets of wax paper. After rolling to desired size, remove top sheet of wax paper, take a table knife and run it around the complete edge of the pie crust so that you have about an inch-wide band loosened—turn the entire crust—with wax paper—over the pie pan and slowly peel off the paper. Flute edges and again with the table knife, cut off the left-over crust on edge of pie pan. If you are making a double-crusted pie, repeat with another piece of the pie crust dough.

Yield: 3—9 inch crusts or 4—8 inch crusts

DOUBLE BONUS: If you just need one pie crust, proceed with the remaining dough, making two more

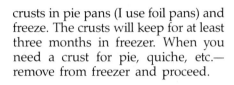

crusts in pie pans (I use foil pans) and freeze. The crusts will keep for at least three months in freezer. When you need a crust for pie, quiche, etc.— remove from freezer and proceed.

If you have a food processor, the pie crust can be made by putting the flour, salt and shortening in processor bowl; using steel blade whirl just until mixture reaches *pebble* stage—pour the egg-vinegar-water mixture slowly through feed tube until ball forms. This will take a very, very short time—about 15 seconds. Proceed as above. . .this is how I make my pie crusts—and I marvel at the simplicity of it all every time I make them.

FRESH STRAWBERRY PIE

When fresh strawberries are at their peak, try this super Fresh Strawberry Pie served with whipped cream—there is no comparison.

3 cups fresh strawberries

Boil 1 cup of the berries with 1 cup water—after three minutes, put through a strainer.

2 tablespoons flour
1 tablespoon cornstarch
¾ cup sugar
1/8 teaspoon salt
¼ cup cold water.

Mix together.
Add this to the hot strawberry juice. Cook until thickened. Place sliced uncooked strawberries in 8-inch baked pie shell. Pour cooked mixture over. Chill well—serve with *real* whipped cream.

SOUR CREAM APPLE PIE

If you like Dutch Apple Pie, you will like Sour Cream Apple Pie even more. The two pies are definitely related to one another.

4 cups peeled, diced
  (finely chopped)
  tart apples
¾ cup granulated sugar
1/8 teaspoon salt
1 egg
2 tablespoons flour
1 teaspoon vanilla
½ teaspoon—grated nutmeg
¼ teaspoon cinnamon
1 cup dairy sour cream

Sift the flour, salt and sugar. Stir into flour mixture the egg, sour cream, vanilla, nutmeg and cinnamon. Beat to a thin batter. Stir in the apples and pour into unbaked pie crust (don't forget *Pie Crust Supreme*).

Bake in 400 degree oven for 15 minutes; reduce heat to 350 degrees and bake another 30 minutes.

SPICY TOPPING:

⅓ cup sugar
⅓ cup flour
1 teaspoon cinnamon
¼ cup butter

Cut together with fork. Remove pie from oven when done; scatter the Spicy Topping on top and return to 400 degree oven for 10 minutes.

Yield: 1—9 inch pie

BONUS: If you are harvesting a good apple crop, you can make, bake and freeze Sour Cream Apple Pies for later consumption. Before serving, thaw and reheat if desired—a big *dollop* of vanilla ice cream is the *tip of the iceberg*.

SACKED APPLE PIE

Definitely sacked—this is a fun pie to make and your oven will remain sparkling clean because the overflow will go into the sack and not on the bottom of the oven. It's tasty, too.

1—unbaked 10-inch pie shell

**5 to 6 large apples,
  peeled and sliced**
¹/₂ cup sugar
2 generous tablespoons flour
**¹/₂ teaspoon grated nutmeg
  (don't get lazy—buy that
  $2.00 grater)**
1 teaspoon cinnamon
2 tablespoons lemon juice

In a large bowl, mix all ingredients well and spoon into unbaked pie shell.

TOPPING:

¹/₂ cup flour
¹/₂ teaspoon cinnamon
¹/₂ cup butter (or margarine)

Combine the flour and cinnamon. Cut in the butter until mixed well—should be *crumbly*. Scatter evenly over pie.

Put the pie in a heavy, brown paper sack. Fold over end of sack a few times to seal.

Place on a cookie sheet and bake in 425 degree oven for 1 hour.

Remove pie from oven, open sack to allow pie to cool.

Yield: 6—8 servings

FRESH HUCKLEBERRY PIE

Enjoy huckleberries at their finest—uncooked and most flavorful and fresh from the bush. This pie combines both cooked and uncooked berries—it is double, double delicious. . .

1 baked 9-inch pie crust

4 cups uncooked huckleberries
3 ounces softened cream cheese
½ cup water
¾ cup sugar
2 tablespoons cornstarch
2 tablespoons fresh lemon juice

Whipped cream for garnish

Cook 1 cup of the berries in ½ cup water. Bring to a boil and reduce heat. Simmer for 2 minutes.

Mix the cornstarch and sugar; gradually add to the berries. Cook— stirring constantly—until thick and clear. Take off heat and cool slightly. Add the lemon juice and complete cooling process.

Line the baked pie shell with cream cheese.

Place the 3 cups of *raw* uncooked huckleberries on top of cream cheese and lastly pour the cooled, cooked berry sauce on top.

BONUS: Before serving—garnish with sweetened whipped cream to which a teaspoon of vanilla has been added.

BANANA CREAM PIE

Unequivocally the best banana cream pie ever! You will never make old-fashioned banana pie again.

1 9-inch baked pie shell

1 3½-ounce package vanilla
  pudding (not instant)
1 envelope unflavored
  gelatin
2¼ cups milk
1 package fluffy white
  frosting mix
1½ teaspoons rum
Dash salt
Fresh grated nutmeg—
  a couple of swoops down
  the grater
3 bananas
1 ounce semisweet chocolate
(1 square)
1 tablespoon butter

In medium saucepan, combine pudding mix and gelatin. Cook according to directions on pudding box, using the 2¼ cups milk.

Remove from heat; cover with piece of waxed paper so *crust* doesn't form on pudding; set aside.

Make frosting according to directions adding the rum, salt and nutmeg.

Fold the hot pudding into the frosting. Slice one banana into pie shell; cover with one-half of the filling. Repeat with second banana and the remaining filling. Chill for 3 to 4 hours.

Just before serving, diagonally slice the remaining banana and arrange on pie. Melt together the square of chocolate and butter, mixing well. Drizzle over banana.

ENJOY!

BONUS: Variety, it is said, is the spice of life. The next time you make a pie crust, add 3 tablespoons finely chopped pecans to the flour mixture before adding the liquid. This crust is a nice addition to any cream pie—and especially Banana Cream Pie.

RHUBARB SURPRISE PIE

*Search no more—here is a most delightful surprise in rhubarb desserts—with an **unrollable** pie crust!*

1 cup all-purpose flour 1 teaspoon baking powder ½ teaspoon salt	Sift together and add:
2 tablespoons butter 1 egg beaten 2 tablespoons milk	Mold dough to a 9-inch pie pan and add:
3 cups diced raw rhubarb 1—3 ounce package strawberry Jello	

TOPPING:

½ cup all-purpose flour 1 cup sugar ½ teaspoon cinnamon ¼ cup melted butter	Mix together and scatter on top of pie: Bake in 350 degree oven for 50 minutes.

VALENTINE'S DAY PIE

*An adventuresome collection of fruits piled high in a meringue shell makes this a **loving** donation to any Valentine's Day celebration.*

One meringue shell:

6 egg whites ½ cup granulated sugar 1 teaspoon cream tartar	Beat the egg whites until soft peaks form. Add the sugar slowly until stiff peaks form. Add cream tartar. In a lightly buttered 10-inch pie plate, spoon the meringue—spreading it upon the sides to form a deep dish pie

shell. Bake in 250 degree oven for one hour. Do not open oven during baking. Meringue should be light golden. Remove from oven and let cool.

FILLING:

1—15-¹/₄ ounce can crushed pineapple (drained well)
4—6 bananas sliced
1 can cherry pie filling
1 cup macadamia nuts—chopped

Cover bottom of cooled shell with filling IN ORDER GIVEN. Chill—at least 3 hours.

Before serving, top with the whipped cream and garnish with coconut.

1 pint whipped cream
1 cup coconut flakes

BONUS: Be sure to serve this pie very cold.

MACADAMIA NUT CREME RUM PIE

I could go on and on with the title of this extraordinarily delicious pie! Suffice it to say—you must try it to believe me and the many others who will clamor for its contents.

¹/₂ cup granulated sugar
1 envelope unflavored gelatin
2 tablespoons cornstarch
¹/₄ teaspoon salt
1—3-ounce package cream cheese
¹/₄ cup dairy sour cream
1¹/₂ cups milk

2 egg yolks—beaten

2 egg whites
3-4 tablespoons rum

2 cups Cool Whip

Mix together in a blender the first seven ingredients. Place in top of double boiler and cook, stirring constantly until thickened - about 5 minutes. Place in top pan of double boiler and cook, stirring constantly, until thick—about 5 minutes.

Whisk some of the hot cooked mixture into the egg yolks and return to the mixture in the double boilder - cook another 3 minutes, remove from heat and cool.

Whip the 2 egg whites until stiff and fold into the cooled filling. Stir in the rum. Chill.

1 - 3½ ounce jar Macademia nuts - chopped

1 - baked 10-inch pie crust (*Pie Crust Supreme*)

Fold the Cool Whip into the chilled filling together with three-fourths of the macadamia nuts. Pour into pie shell, and chill.

Before serving—garnish with whipped cream and remaining nuts.

Yield: 6—8 servings

BONUS: Before serving—whip 1 cup whipping cream and pipe around edge of pie, sprinkle with remaining nuts. This really gives the pie a professional, polished attitude—your guests will applaud your talents.

DAR'S MUD PIE

*I became acquainted with Mud Pie in Hawaii . . . since that acquaintance I have had the pleasure of **test tasting** the abundancy of Mud Pies in existence. Dar's Mud Pie is a culmination of all that tasting . . .*

CRUST:

12 Oreo cookies crushed (use blender or food processor)
3 tablespoons melted butter

1 quart (plus) coffee ice cream

Combine cookie crumbs and butter and press into bottom of buttered 9—10-inch pie pan. Refrigerate. When chilled, spoon one-half softened ice cream on top of crust. Pour half of Mud Sauce over ice cream and proceed with another layer of ice cream and top off with the remaining Mud Sauce.

MUD SAUCE:

1 cup Nestle's semi-sweet chocolate chips

In medium sauce pan, melt the sauce ingredients over medium heat, stirring

1 cup miniature
  marshmallows
1 cup evaporated milk
1 teaspoon vanilla

constantly until mixture thickens, adding vanilla after removing sauce from heat. Cool long enough so as to not melt the ice cream while pouring Mud Sauce over it. Top with Garnish and freeze.

GARNISH:

1 cup whipping cream—
  whipped
2 ounces Kahlua liqueur
1/4 cup powdered sugar
1/2 cups chopped nuts

Whip cream, add powdered sugar and Kahlua. Decorate top of Mud Pie with Garnish—use decorating bag with star or shell tip—or spread whipped cream over pie and sprinkle top with finely chopped nuts. Freeze solid.

BONUS: Double the recipe and use a 9x13-inch buttered pan. This will serve 24 persons. Also if you do not like the idea of nuts on top of the whipped cream Garnish, use chocolate curls or shavings.

SHAVINGS: Use a block of chocolate (thick hunk of chocolate or candy bar) and with a *potato* peeler, peel the chocolate along one of the edges—it will make super chocolate curls— chocolate should be room temperature—if you use a cold piece of chocolate you will get bits and pieces of shavings.

FUDGE SUNDAE PIE

You can conjure up this delicious ice cream pie like magic. It is such a satisfying treat that it, too, will magically disappear.

1 cup evaporated milk
1 cup Nestles semi-sweet
   chocolate morsels
1 cup miniature
   marshmallows
¼ teaspoon salt
1 teaspoon vanilla

Mix together ingredients in heavy one-quart saucepan. Over medium heat, stir until chocolate chips and marshmallows melt completely and mixture thickens. Remove from heat and cool to room temperature.

Line bottom and sides of 9-inch pie pan with whole vanilla wafers.

Spoon softened vanilla ice cream over the wafers, spoon with half of the fudge sauce. Repeat with more ice cream and spoon remaining fudge sauce on top.

Sprinkle chopped nuts on top of fudge pie if desired. Freeze solid— at least 6 hours.

Yield: 6—8 servings

BONUS: Use any flavor ice cream— i.e., peppermint, coffee, chocolate or any combination.
Also, the fudge sauce makes a delicious hot fudge topping. It can be refrigerated and reheated for that bedtime snack.

OLD-FASHIONED LEMON MERINGUE PIE

Looking for that extra-special something to serve your card club or special dinner guests? Serve this nutritious lemon cream pie.

1 9-inch baked pie shell

1 cup sugar
5 tablespoons cornstarch
1/4 teaspoon salt
2 cups milk
3 egg yolks
3 tablespoons butter
1 teaspoon grated lemon
   peel
1/3 cup fresh lemon juice

MERINGUE:

3 egg whites
1/4 teaspoon salt
1 teaspoon lemon juice
1/4 teaspoon vanilla
6 tablespoons sugar

In a medium saucepan, mix the sugar, cornstarch and salt. Gradually add the milk, stirring until smooth. Cook over medium-low heat, stirring constantly until smooth and thickened—about 10 minutes. Stir a small amount of the hot mixture into the egg yolks. Gradually add the yolks with the remaining hot mixture, cooking an additional 4 minutes, stirring constantly. Remove from heat—add the butter, lemon peel and juice. Stir to blend thoroughly. Set aside and prepare the meringue.

In mixer bowl, add salt, vanilla and juice to the egg whites. Beat until foamy. Add sugar one tablespoon at a time, beating constantly until sugar is dissolved and whites become glossy and stand in soft peaks.

Pour the hot filling into baked pie shell. Spread meringue on pie filling, starting with small amounts at edges and build up to middle of pie. Be certain that meringue covers all of pie including its edges—spread in attractive swirls.

Bake pie in 350 degree oven for 12—15 minutes or until tips of meringue are light golden. Cool on rack before serving.

BONUS: The lemon filling can be

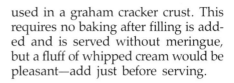

used in a graham cracker crust. This requires no baking after filling is added and is served without meringue, but a fluff of whipped cream would be pleasant—add just before serving.

MOCHA ALASKA PIE

*There is nothing more fun to serve than a **Baked Alaska** dessert. Mocha Alaska Pie is no exception to the rule—it is **scrummy**, too.*

1 cup Nabisco vanilla creme filled cookie crumbs
¼ cup melted butter

Combine and press evenly over bottom and sides of 9-inch pie pan. Bake for 10 minutes in 350 degree oven.

1 quart slightly softened coffee or mocha flavored ice cream. Spoon into cooled crust and freeze until firm.

Beat egg whites until frothy, add vanilla and cream of tartar and beat until soft peaks form.

1—5½ ounce can chocolate syrup drizzled evenly over ice cream. ½ cups chopped nuts sprinkled over top of chocolate drizzle. Freeze until firm.

6 tablespoons sugar—add one tablespoon at a time and continue beating 1 minute after each addition until stiff peaks form.

3 egg whites
½ teaspoon vanilla
¼ teaspoon cream of tartar

Swirl meringue evenly over pie, sealing to edge of crust. Return pie to freezer.

When frozen, wrap lightly but airtight. To serve—place uncovered frozen pie in 450 degree oven for 4 minutes or until meringue is golden. WATCH THIS PROCESS CAREFULLY.

Yield: 8 servings

BONUS: Obviously this dessert can be prepared well in advance of that big dinner party and popped in the oven for that fresh *Alaska* look. This is fun just to prepare for your own family—the kids will love it.

BLUM'S COFFEE TOFFEE PIE

Blum's of San Francisco fame, used to serve a Coffee-Toffee pie that was ineffable. I have made this sinfully luscious dessert over the years and it is the one most requested by **repeater** *dinner guests and the one most likened to coffee-toffee pie made famous by Blum's.*

Pastry shell:

½ **package piecrust mix**
¼ **cup light-brown sugar, firmly packed**
¾ **cup finely chopped walnuts**
1 **square unsweetened chocolate, grated**
1 **teaspoon vanilla**

Filling:

½ **cup soft unsalted butter**
¾ **cup granulated sugar**
1 **square unsweetened chocolate, melted and cooled**
2 **teaspoons instant coffee (powdered)**
2 **eggs**

Topping:

2 **cups whipping cream**
2 **tablespoons instant coffee (Espresso powder is best)**
½ **cup confectioners' sugar**
Chocolate curls

Make Pastry shell—in medium bowl, combine piecrust mix with brown sugar, walnuts and grated chocolate. Add 1 tablespoon water and the vanilla; using fork mix until well blended. Turn into well buttered 9-inch pie plate; press firmly against bottom and sides of pie plate. Bake 15 minutes. Cool on wire rack.

Meanwhile, make Filling—in small bowl, with electric mixer at medium speed, beat the butter until it is creamy.
Gradually add granulated sugar, beating until light. Blend in cool melted chocolate and 2 teaspoons instant coffee.
Add 1 egg; beat 5 minutes. Add second egg; beat 5 minutes longer. Turn filling into baked pie shell. Refrigerate the pie, covered at least 8 hours but best held overnight.

Topping—next day make topping—in large bowl, combine cream with 2 tablespoons instant coffee and the confectioners' sugar. Cover and refrigerate 1 hour.
Beat cream mixture until stiff. Decorate pie with topping, using pastry bag with star or shell decorating tip, if desired. Garnish with chocolate curls. Refrigerate the pie at least 2 hours.

STRAWBERRY CHEESECAKE PIE

A combination of frozen and fresh strawberries blended over a
cheesecake-like *pie crust makes this strawberry pie one-of-a-kind.*
If you are not particularly fond of fresh strawberry pie—this will
be a more than pleasant surprise to your taste buds.

1 baked 10-inch pie shell

**1—8 ounce package cream
cheese**
**1—4 ounce package cream
cheese**
**⅓ cup small curd creamed
cottage cheese**
¼ teaspoon salt
½ cup granulated sugar
2 eggs
2 teaspoons vanilla

With a mixer on low speed blend the
cottage cheese, cream cheese and
vanilla.
Add sugar and the eggs, one at a time.
Mix at medium speed until well
blended.
Pour into a 10-inch baked pie shell and
bake at 350 degrees for 20—25
minutes.
Let cool until set.

MEANWHILE:

Make the strawberry filling:
**2—10-ounce packages frozen,
sliced strawberries, thawed**
¼ cup sugar
¼ cup lemon juice
4 tablespoons corn starch
1—2 drops red food coloring

Mix the sugar and corn starch with ¼
cup strawberry juice and mix well. Put
rest of strawberries in sauce pan, adding corn starch— sugar mixture,
lemon juice. Mix well. Cook this over
medium heat until thick and clear.
Cool and pour over cheese filling.
Then arrange 1 quart whole fresh
strawberries over top (stem sides
down). Chill 1—2 hours and serve
with whipped cream if desired.

Yield: 6—8 servings

CHEESECAKE KITTREDGE

*No cookbook would be complete without Cheesecake—and this is extraordinarily **cheesy** - it utilizes more than just the inevitable cream cheese. If you are looking for something new in cheesecakes, I need not expound beyond this prelude.*

*1 pound Farmer's cheese
1—8 ounce package cream
cheese
2 cups sugar (or 1¾ cups)
6 egg yolks

½ pint heavy cream
(old-fashioned whipping
cream will work)
3 tablespoons cornstarch
1 teaspoon vanilla
6 egg whites—beaten stiff
1 box Nabisco Zwieback—
moistened with not quite
¼ pound butter and
½ cup granulated sugar.

Butter a 9 or 10 inch springform pan and line it with the zwieback crumb mixture. Reserve a portion to cover top of cake.

Beat the cheeses until very creamy. (I ran the Farmer's cheese through the shredder of my food processor to prepare it for *creaming* with the cream cheese).
Add sugar and egg yolks and beat well.

Dissolve cornstarch in the cream. Fold in the beaten egg whites. Add to cheese mixture.
Pour into shell. Sprinkle top with reserved crumb mixture.

Bake in 325 degree oven for 70 minutes (1 hour plus 10 minutes). Allow to cool in oven.

To appreciate cheesecake at its *peak* - serve the next day.

BONUS: *Farmer, pot and cottage cheeses are all domestically produced *fresh* cheeses. Generally, pot cheese is most similar to cottage cheese, but it contains less moisture and is never *creamed*. Farmer cheese is drier and firmer and is pressed into loaf shapes—thus called *pressed* OR *farm* cheese in some areas. Farmer's cheese

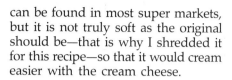

can be found in most super markets, but it is not truly soft as the original should be—that is why I shredded it for this recipe—so that it would cream easier with the cream cheese.

MERINGUED RHUBARB

Meringued Rhubarb is an interesting variation of Rhubarb Betty. For those of us who find rhubarb a rare treat—the meringue increases the delectation of this Springtime rhizome.

CRUST:

1½ cubes margarine or butter
2 cups flour

Mix together and press in 9 x 13 inch pan. BAKE at 350 degrees for 10 minutes. Cool slightly.

6 egg yolks
1 cup evaporated milk
1½ cups sugar (or more)
4 tablespoons flour
Pinch of salt
5 cups fresh rhubarb—cut in fine cubes (food processor works great)

Mix egg yolks, etc. Stir in Rhubarb.

BAKE at 350 degrees for 45 minutes. Remove from oven and cool slightly.

MERINGUE TOPPING:

Beat 6 egg whites until frothy
Add 12 tablespoons sugar—
2 at a time
1 teaspoon vanilla
Beat until stiff

SPREAD MERINGUE TOPPING over baked Rhubarb—covering completely. BAKE 10 minutes at 350 degrees. Cool before serving.

RHUBARB A LA CRUNCH

1 cup all-purpose flour
1 cup brown sugar
1 cup oatmeal (Quick
   Quaker Oats is acceptable)
½ cup melted shortening
   (use ¼ cup butter and
   ¼ cup Butter Crisco)
1 teaspoon cinnamon

4 cups diced rhubarb

1⅓ cups granulated sugar
1 cup water
2 teaspoons cornstarch
1 teaspoon vanilla

Mix together flour, oatmeal, brown sugar, shortening and cinnamon until crumbly.

In a 9-inch square pan, pour one-half of the crumbly mixture, pat lightly with heel of hand or fork.
Spoon the diced rhubarb on top of crumbly mixture.

COMBINE:

Granulated sugar, water, cornstarch and vanilla. Cook over low heat until *clear*. Pour this over the rhubarb and top with remaining crumblies.

Bake in 350 degree oven for 1 hour.

BONUS: The *clear* cooked sauce is an innovation, and certainly enhances the customary, every-day CRUNCH— whether it be apple, cranberry or rhubarb.

APPLE CRISP GRANT

No recipe manual can be perfected without an old-fashioned Apple Crisp between the covers . . . Apple Crisp Grant is that perfection.

1 cup brown sugar,
   firmly packed
½ cup all-purpose flour
½ teaspoon cinnamon
½ teaspoon freshly grated
   nutmeg
¼ teaspoon salt
¼ cup butter or margarine
5 cups sliced apples (5 to 6)

Mix together sugar, flour, spices and salt. Cut in the butter until mixture is *crumbly*.

Spread the apples in a buttered 8 or 9-inch square baking pan.
Scatter crumbly mixture over fruit, pat lightly with fork.

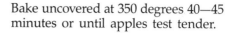

Bake uncovered at 350 degrees 40—45 minutes or until apples test tender.

BONUS: Best served warm with a dollop of whipped cream—or vanilla ice cream. Take your pick from whatever you have on hand. It is, however, delicious without the *fringes*.

DOUBLE DECADENCE MUFFINS

*A real double **threat** are these chocolate cupcakes. For you chocolate lovers—here is the true chocolate treat you have been waiting for.*

Sift together:

2½ cups all-purpose flour
2 teaspoons baking powder
½ teaspoon salt
½ cup cocoa

With an electric beater:

1½ cups milk
1 egg
½ cup melted butter
½ cup granulated sugar

Mix well and pour into the flour mixture.

Stir in:

½ cup chocolate chips
½ cup chopped nuts
Cream cheese

Spoon batter into greased muffin pan—not quite half full. Place about 1 teaspoon cream cheese on top of batter, then cover with more of the batter.

Bake in 350 degree oven for 20—25 minutes—test for doneness.

While still warm dip tops of cupcakes in some melted butter and then in a mixture of cinnamon and granulated sugar.

BONUS: The muffins are very rich so they might spill over the edge of the cups somewhat.

ESPRESSO CHARLOTTE

*A cappuccino-like, extravagant dessert wrapped in chocolate dipped ladyfingers—there will be no **turn downs**.*

2 envelopes unflavored
  gelatin
½ cup cold strong coffee
1½ cups hot strong coffee
1 cup sugar

1—6 ounce package
  semisweet chocolate chips
3—3 ounce packages
  ladyfingers, split
  lengthwise in half

2 cups whipping cream
1 tablespoon vanilla

½ cup whipping cream
Chopped or sliced almonds

Soften gelatin in ½ cup cold coffee in small saucepan. Stir in 1 ½ cups hot coffee and the sugar; beat over low heat until gelatin dissolves. Refrigerate until mixture is consistency of unbeaten egg whites—about ½ hour.

Melt chocolate in top of double boiler over simmering water. Dip 1 end of 16 ladyfinger halves into chocolate; reserve remaining ladyfingers. Place dipped ladyfingers on baking sheet and refrigerate uncovered until chocolate hardens—about 10—15 minutes.

Beat 2 cups cream in large mixer bowl until stiff; add the vanilla. Fold into gelatin mixture.

Spread 1-inch layer of filling in 9-inch springform pan. Line side with dipped ladyfingers—cut side in—chocolate tip up. Pour one-third of remaining filling into pan and top with half of the reserved ladyfingers; repeat—top with remaining filling. Refrigerate at least 6 hours.

Before serving—beat ½ cup whipping cream in small bowl until stiff. Pipe whipped cream on top of—or if you do not have a pastry bag with decorative tips—spread whipped cream on top of charlotte. Place on serving plate—or footed cake plate—remove side of pan. Sprinkle with almonds.

Yield: Serves 12

BONUS: If you cannot find ladyfingers in your local bakery you can
make your own. Please see *Homemade
Ladyfingers* - in Dessert section of *Best
of Friends, etc.*

RHUBARB CAKE MARY

*If you find a cache of rhubarb and are overwhelmed with it, by it
and of it—Rhubarb Cake Mary will alleviate some of that
apprehension.*

1½ **cups granulated sugar**
½ **cup solid shortening**
1 egg
1 teaspoon vanilla
**1 cup sour milk (1 teaspoon
vinegar stirred into *sweet*
milk)**
**2—3 cups rhubarb—finely
chopped or sliced**
2 cups all-purpose flour
1 teaspoon soda

Cream the shortening and sugar; add
egg and vanilla
Add milk—then add the flour and
soda all at once. Blend thoroughly.
Hand-fold in the rhubarb.

Pour into a 9x13-inch cake pan which
has been greased and floured.
Sprinkle on topping.

TOPPING:

⅓ **cup granulated sugar**
1 teaspoon cinnamon

Combine and sprinkle evenly over top
of cake batter before baking.

Bake in a 350 degree oven for 40—50
minutes.

BONUS: *Mary* uses Butter-flavored
Crisco for the shortening above.

TRIFLE DE FETE

Presentation of trifles vary—but all include custard, fruit, whipped cream, pound cake or ladyfingers soaked with rum or other liquor. Trifle de Fete **gorgeously encased with ribbon** *and presented on a footed cake plate is definitely* **blue ribbon** *fare.*

½ cup sugar
¼ cup all-purpose flour
2¼ cups milk
4 egg yolks—beaten
2 teaspoons shredded lemon peel
2 teaspoons vanilla

2—3 ounce packages ladyfingers, split or
24 *Homemade Ladyfingers* (see *Homemade Ladyfingers - Best of Friends, etc.*)

¼ cup rum
1½ cups fresh strawberries (sliced)—reserve some for garnish
1½ cups pineapple chunks

2 cups whipping cream
¼ cup powdered sugar
1 teaspoon vanilla
1 tablespoon chocolate

Pudding: In a saucepan combine the ½ cup sugar and flour. Stir in milk, beaten egg yolks and lemon peel. Cook and stir over medium heat until thickened and bubbly. Cook and stir 1 minute more. Remove from heat; stir in the 2 teaspoons vanilla. Cool.

Sprinkle half the ladyfingers with half of the rum; arrange on bottom and side of a 9-inch springform pan. Top with sliced strawberries. Spoon half of pudding atop strawberries. Arrange remaining ladyfingers on top; sprinkle with remaining rum.
Place pineapple chunks over ladyfingers; top with remaining pudding. Chill at least 6 hours—or overnight.

One hour before serving, pour the two cups of cream into mixer bowl, stirring in the powdered sugar. Place covered in refrigerator for ½ hour. Whip the cream, adding vanilla—until stiff enough to pipe through pastry bag fitted with star or shell tip. Decorate top of Trifle and garnish with reserved strawberries.

Transfer to serving plate, carefully remove edge of pan. At this point add a 1 ½-inch colorful grosgrain ribbon by *wrapping* around the Trifle de Fete—

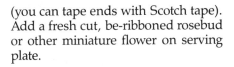

(you can tape ends with Scotch tape). Add a fresh cut, be-ribboned rosebud or other miniature flower on serving plate.

Yield: 10—12 generous servings

BONUS: Any combination of fruit can be used. Fresh raspberries together with fresh peeled and chopped peaches are delicious. Use canned, drained fruit if fresh fruits of your choice are unavailable.

GEN'S BAKED CHOCOLATE PUDDING

For the **chocoholic** *- a temptation no one can resist. Gen's Baked Chocolate Pudding deserves a* **gold star** *rating.*

1 square unsweetened
   chocolate, melted
2 tablespoons melted butter
¾ cup granulated sugar
¼ teaspoon salt
1 teaspoon vanilla
1 cup all-purpose flour
2 teaspoons baking powder
½ cup milk
½ cup chopped walnuts

½ cup granulated sugar
½ cup brown sugar
4 tablespoons cocoa

Combine the chocolate, butter, salt and vanilla in saucepan in which the chocolate was melted. Add sifted dry ingredients alternately with the milk. Stir in walnuts. Pour into an 8-inch round greased pan and top with the sugars and cocoa mixture.

Pour 1 cup of water over all.

Bake in 350 degree oven for 40 minutes or until center tests *set*.

Serve warm with plain cream or whipped cream.

BONUS: The pudding doubles nicely.

APRICOT JAM STRUDEL

*Whenever I see **strudel** connected with a recipe, I generally skip over it because the strudel dough is too tedious and time-consuming to prepare. The dough for Apricot Jam Strudel is a pleasant surprise and the final result highlights any occasion.*

½ cup unsalted butter
2 cups all-purpose flour
¼ teaspoon salt
1 cup dairy sour cream

Mix first four ingredients—as for piecrust. Let stand overnight in refrigerator.

Next day, let stand at room temperature. Divide dough into two parts, and on lightly floured board, roll each half into rectangle about 15x7-inches.

1 10 ounce jar apricot jam (use homemade if you have on hand)
1 cup shredded coconut
⅔ cup finely chopped nuts (pecans or walnuts)

Combine and spread over the dough

Lap over until dough is about 15x3-inches. (Does not roll easily as it is a rich dough—fold over carefully). Place seam-side down on baking sheet.

Bake at 350 degrees for 1 hour. Remove from oven, cool 10 minutes. Sprinkle with confectioners' sugar. Cut in ½ inch slices.

Yield: 2 strudels

BONUS: I have frozen the baked strudel and it keeps very well. It is nice to have on hand for unexpected *drop-in's* or *drop-outs*.

BROKEN GLASS TORTE

*A very colorful and soothing dessert—well received after a multifarious dinner. Also doubles as that something special to serve to the **bridge club**.*

MIXTURE NO. 1:

1 package each of three different flavors Jello
1½ cups hot water for each package.

Mix each flavor in its separate bowl and pour into square pans. When set, cut into ½ inch squares.

MIXTURE NO. 2:

2 envelopes unflavored gelatin

Dissolve in ¼ cup cold water.
Add 1 cup hot pineapple juice. Let this cool until just starting to set.

MIXTURE NO. 3:

2 cups whipping cream
½ cup sugar
1 teaspoon vanilla

Fold Mixture No. 2 into Mixture No. 3. Then fold in Jello cubes (Mixture No. 1) carefully.
Spoon into 9x13 inch cake pan which has been lined with two-thirds of Crust Mixture. Disperse remaining crust crumbles over top of Broken Glass Torte. Refrigerate at least 8—12 hours.

CRUST MIXTURE:

2 dozen graham crackers
½ cup softened butter
½ cup granulated sugar

Cut together with a fork.

Yield: Cut in desirable squares.

BONUS: Broken Glass Torte may be made day ahead. Keeps well for several days.
Also, vanilla wafers can be substituted for graham crackers for the Crust.

CHOCOLATE BANANA LOAF

This Chocolate Banana Loaf is more a cake than a bread—thus categorized under desserts. Whatever—it is delicious for breakfast, tea, or as a bedtime snack.

8 ounces unsweetened
  baking chocolate,
  coarsely chopped
1 cup butter,
  room temperature
4 cups granulated sugar
4 eggs
1½ cups banana puree,
  made from 4 very, very
  ripe bananas
1½ cups milk
2 tablespoons vanilla
4 cups self-rising flour
1 teaspoon cinnamon
2 cups chopped pecans

Melt the chocolate in top of double boiler over hot but not boiling water. Remove from heat and cool.
Beat butter in large bowl of an electric mixer. Add the sugar, 2 tablespoons at a time—beat until fluffy. Beat in the eggs one at a time and then the melted chocolate.

Combine banana puree, milk and vanilla. Alternately add the flour and cinnamon and the banana milk liquid to the chocolate mixture— beginning and ending with flour. Fold in the pecans.

Pour the batter into 3 greased and floured 9x5x2 ½-inch loaf pans and bake 45—50 minutes. Loaves will pull away from sides of pan when done. Remove from oven, cool on rack for 15 minutes. Turn loaves out of pans and frost with chocolate/coffee glaze.

CHOCOLATE/COFFEE GLAZE:

1 cup powdered sugar
2 tablespoons hot coffee
1 teaspoon vanilla
1 tablespoon cocoa

Beat together to a thin glaze consistency. Drizzle over banana loaves while still warm.

BONUS: Extra loaves freeze perfectly.

CHOCOLATE STEAM PUDDING

*A Sheridan-McCabe family favorite served by them during the winter and for holidays and birthdays. You, too, will want to include this steam pudding in your **favorites** file.*

⅓ **cup butter**
¾ **cup sugar**
2 **eggs**
⅔ **cup milk**
1½ **cups cake flour**
1 **teaspoon baking powder**
2 **squares unsweetened chocolate, melted.**

Cream the butter and sugar.
Separate the eggs and add yolks to the creamed mixture.
Sift the cake flour with baking powder and add alternately with milk.
Carefully blend in melted chocolate.
In a small bowl beat the egg whites until stiff—then fold into the cake mixture.
Pour into a greased mold. Place covered mold in a large pan filled one-fourth full of water and cover with lid. Make certain mold is slightly elevated off steamer bottom.
Steam for 1¼ hours.

SAUCE FOR CHOCOLATE STEAM PUDDING

2 **tablespoons butter**
1 **cup powdered sugar**
1 **egg**

Cream together.

When smooth, add a pinch of salt and 1 teaspoon vanilla.

Just before serving fold in ½ pint of cream—whipped.

Yield: 8 servings

BONUS: Get out of the cake and pie routine and serve this delicious pudding. Many of you have probably never prepared a steam pudding—go for it—this one is fool-proof.

CHOCOLATE ROLL

*A **devastatingly** delicious chocolate cake roll. Don't shy away from this because you **don't do** roll cakes. It is surprisingly easy to make and an extra-special treat for everyone.*

CAKE:

5 eggs (separated)

Sift:

¾ cup powdered sugar
2 tablespoons flour
2 rounded tablespoons cocoa
powder
1/8 teaspoon salt

2 tablespoons vanilla

Separate the eggs. Beat whites until stiff—beat the yolks until light yellow and creamy. Blend the two together and add the sifted ingredients. Add vanilla.

Pour batter into a well greased, wax-paper lined cookie sheet.

Bake at 400 degrees for 5—7 minutes.

Turn out on a powder-sugared towel and roll. Allow to cool. Unroll and spread with FILLING.

FILLING:

1 cup whipping cream
¼ cup powdered sugar
½ teaspoon vanilla

Whip the cream, add the sugar and vanilla. Spread on roll.

Reroll the cake. Serve with WARM SAUCE.

SAUCE:

1 cup granulated sugar
1 tablespoon cocoa
3 tablespoons flour
2 cups milk
2 tablespoons butter
½ teaspoon vanilla
½ cup chopped nuts

Mix the dry ingredients. Slowly add milk and cook until mixture thickens. Add vanilla and nuts.

Slice the Chocolate Roll in desired servings—spoon warm sauce over slices, or put the Sauce in a *sauce-boat* and let everyone spoon their own.

CHOCOLATE SHEET CAKE

*This variation of the **inexhaustible** chocolate sheet cake has been proven **favorite** by my **chocoholic** standards.*

Heat in saucepan:

2 sticks margarine
1 cup water
4 tablespoons cocoa powder

Mix in large mixing bowl the above with:

2 cups all-purpose flour
2 cups granulated sugar
1 teaspoon soda
2 teaspoons cinnamon

Blend well and add:

2 eggs
2 teaspoons vanilla
½ cup buttermilk

FROSTING:
¼ cup buttermilk
½ stick margarine
3 tablespoons cocoa
1 teaspoon vanilla
2 cups powdered sugar

Mix all ingredients until well blended and pour into a greased and floured Jelly Roll pan—cookie sheet with sides.

Bake 350 degrees for 30 minutes—test for doneness. Remove from oven and cool on wire rack 15 minutes before frosting.

BONUS: Sprinkle frosting with finely chopped nuts or chocolate sprinkles—I like to do half of each—for those who do not like nuts, the chocolate sprinkles are fun—or just leave plain. If you do not need to serve entire cake, cut in squares, wrap and freeze—it does not dry out like a lot of frozen cakes. This is an easy and quick cake to make—just dig out a wooden spoon and mix away—you do not need a *mixer.*

ZUCCHINI CHOCOLATE CAKE

*The prolific zucchini teems with a variety of usages. It is a **triple-threat** - you can serve it as a vegetable, cooked or in a salad, as a bread and finally as a chocolate cake.*

½ **cup margarine, room**
  temperature
½ **cup vegetable oil**
1¾ **cups granulated sugar**
2 **eggs**
½ **cup sour milk**
1 **teaspoon vanilla**

1½ **cups all-purpose flour**
½ **teaspoon baking powder**
1 **teaspoon baking soda**
4 **tablespoons cocoa**
½ **teaspoon cinnamon**
½ **teaspoon cloves**

2 **cups grated zucchini**
  (unpeeled)
½ **cup chocolate chips**

Cream the margarine, oil and sugar. Add eggs, vanilla and milk. Beat with mixer until well-blended.
Mix dry ingredients and add to creamed mixture. Beat well.
Stir in the zucchini and pour into greased and floured 9x12 loaf pan or two smaller pans.
Sprinkle the chocolate chips on atop.

Bake in 325 degree oven for 40—45 minutes.

BONUS: I use two smaller loaf pans—eat one pronto and freeze the second for a rainy day.

MY FAVORITE CHOCOLATE CAKE
(with filling)

*I am a profound **chocoholic** and this cake together with the filling is absolutely the best method of curbing my intense chocolate craving. The cake, too, is incomparable!*

1 **cup granulated sugar**
4 **tablespoons solid vegetable**
  shortening
2 **eggs**

1½ **cups cake flour**

In large mixer bowl combine and *cream* the first three ingredients.

Sift flour, salt and baking soda

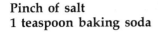

Pinch of salt
1 teaspoon baking soda

½ cup sour milk
(add 1 teaspoon vinegar
or 1 teaspoon lemon juice
to fresh milk to make it
sour).

½ cup boiling water
4 tablespoons cocoa
1 teaspoon vanilla

FILLING:

1 cup granulated sugar
1 tablespoon flour
Dash of salt
½ cup milk
1 egg

**Mix and cook over medium
heat until mixture reaches
bubbly stage and thickens.
Remove from heat and add:**

1 tablespoon butter
1 teaspoon vanilla
½ cup chopped pecans or
walnuts

together and slowly add to cake
mixture.

Mix the boiling water, cocoa and
vanilla together and slowly add to cake
mixture.

Pour batter into two round 9-inch cake
pans—greased and floured.

Bake at 350 degrees for 25—30
minutes. Check for doneness and
remove from oven, cool about 10
minutes and turn out on racks to completely cool.

Spread filling on top of bottom layer
and frost the cake with your favorite
chocolate frosting.

BONUS: Filling is good for any kind
of cake, but is particularly scrumptious
with chocolate.

FRESH APPLE CAKE

By combining ingredients from two excellent fresh apple cake recipes, Fresh Apple Cake was born.

3 cups all-purpose flour
1½ teaspoons baking soda
3 cups pared and finely
   chopped tart apples
½ cup chopped walnuts or
   pecans
1 teaspoon grated lemon peel
2 cups granulated sugar
½ teaspoon salt
1½ cups salad oil
2 eggs
Cream cheese frosting

In a small bowl, combine the apples, ½ cup chopped nuts and the lemon peel.

In large mixing bowl, combine the sugar, salad oil and eggs; beat well with wooden spoon. Add the flour, baking soda and salt—mixing until smooth.

Add apple mixture, stir until well combined, spread evenly into three 9-inch round layer cake pans.

Bake in 350 degree oven 30—40 minutes. Test for doneness. Remove from oven, cool 10 minutes, remove from pans and cool thoroughly on wire racks. Frost.

FROSTING:

1—8 ounce package cream
   cheese, softened
1 tablespoon butter, softened
1 teaspoon vanilla
1 pound confectioner's sugar

In medium bowl with portable mixer on medium speed, beat the cheese, butter and vanilla until light and creamy; add confectioner's sugar and beat until of spreading consistency. Makes 2½ cups frosting.

BONUS: Use a greased and floured 9x13-inch baking pan and instead of frosting, mix together:

½ cups sugar
1 tablespoon butter
1 teaspoon cinnamon
½ cup chopped nuts

Sprinkle on top of cake before baking. Can then be served with Cool Whip if desired.

SPICY HUCKLEBERRY CAKE

For those of us who have huckleberries in the larder—this is a delightfully-delicious use of them!

½ cup butter, softened
1 cup granulated sugar
2 eggs
2 cups all-purpose flour
2 teaspoons baking powder
1 teaspoon each ground cinnamon and grated orange peel
½ teaspoon each baking soda, salt and ground cloves
2 cups fresh or frozen (defrosted) huckleberries
½ cup fresh orange juice
1 teaspoon vanilla

ORANGE GLAZE:

Blend ½ cup unsifted powdered sugar and 1½ tablespoons orange juice until smooth.

Beat butter and sugar until creamy. Add eggs one at a time, beating after each addition.

Combine flour, baking powder, cinnamon, orange peel, soda, salt and cloves; mix ¼ cup flour mixture with berries and reserve.

Beat remaining flour mixture into butter mixture alternately with orange juice until blended; stir in berry mixture and vanilla.

Turn batter into a greased flour-dusted 10 cup tube pan. (Fluted tube pan makes most attractive presentation).

Bake in 350 degree oven for 50 minutes or until pick inserted in center comes out clean.

Cool in pan 10 minutes; invert onto rack, drizzle with glaze.

Yield: Serves 12

BONUS: Blueberries can replace the huckleberries if they are unavailable. Also—the cake freezes well.

HUCKLEBERRY WALNUT CREAM CAKE

Huckleberries are one of Montana's treasures and Huckleberry Walnut Cream Cake adapts well to it. It is truly delectable. Beware, calorie counters.

1½ cups whipping cream
2 teaspoons vanilla
3 eggs
1½ cups flour
1½ cups sugar
1 cup finely chopped
   walnuts
2 teaspoons baking powder
¼ teaspoon salt
1 cup huckleberries

LEMON FROSTING:

1 cup butter
(don't substitute)
3 cups powdered sugar
2 tablespoons lemon juice
1 teaspoon vanilla
4 egg yolks

Beat the cream until stiff, add vanilla. Beat eggs until thickened; fold into whipped cream. Mix dry ingredients and fold into whipped cream mixture. Fold in walnuts and huckleberries.

Pour into two greased and floured 9-inch round or square cake pans.

Bake in 350 degree oven for 30 minutes.

Cool 10 minutes, remove from pans, cool completely on racks.
Beat butter, sugar, juice and vanilla. Beat in egg yolks one at a time until fluffy. Spread between layers and on top of cake. Refrigerate until serving time.

Yield: 12 servings

BONUS: If square baking pans are used, cut cake in half after frosting, and frost cut sides. You will then have two smaller cakes and can freeze one. The cake is very rich and by dividing into two smaller *loaf* cakes, slicing and dividing is less cumbersome.

HARVEY WALLBANGER CAKE

Harvey was, and still is, a very popular fellow! I don't remember where I got the recipe but it remains a favorite among my peers and for those of you who have not had the pleasure—meet Harvey Wallbanger...

1 box **Yellow cake mix**
(or Orange, if you
can find)
1—3 ounce package instant
vanilla pudding mix
4 eggs
1/2 cup vegetable oil
2 ounces Galliano
2 ounces Vodka
1 cup fresh squeezed
orange juice

In a large mixer bowl, beat all ingredients on medium speed for 4 minutes.

Pour batter into a prepared 10 cup Bundt pan or tube cake pan. Bake in 350 degree oven for 40—50 minutes.

Remove from oven, cool 20 minutes, remove from cake pan and Glaze.

GLAZE:

1 cup powdered sugar
(add a bit more if glaze
is too thin)
1 tablespoon Galliano
1 tablespoon vodka
2 tablespoons orange juice

Mix together and drizzle over Harvey!

BONUS: Harvey likes the freezer—so if you have two mini Bundt or tube pans—you can gobble down one and freeze the other. The Galliano and Vodka are the secrets of the cake. Don't omit. If you want a dull cake—just use an unadroited cake mix and be done with it—and don't tell Harvey.

KONA COFFEE MOCHA PUFFS

*Authentically Hawaiian—the **puffs** fulfill that fetish for both coffee and chocolate. I **ferreted** the ingredients while in Hawaii.*

½ cup water
¼ cup butter
½ cup sifted all-purpose flour
2 eggs
4 Mars almond bars chopped (or 8 Fun-size bars)
¼ cup hot coffee (very strong—Kona if available)
½ pint whipping cream

Heat water and butter to boiling in a saucepan. Add flour all at once. Stir rapidly over heat until mixture forms a ball and follows spoon around the pan.

Add eggs—one at a time, beating until mixture is smooth.

(This procedure is similar to any cream puff dough).

Press mixture through a pastry bag into 18 small mounds, 2 inches apart on cookie sheet.

Bake in 400 degree oven for 30 minutes or until puffed and browned. Remove from oven and remove immediately from cookie sheet.

Melt the candy bars with the coffee in a small sauce pan over very low heat. Cool.

Beat the whipping cream until stiff. Fold one-half of the melted bars mixture into the whipped cream.

Split the puffs, fill with the whipped cream-candy bar mixture. Pile puffs on a doilie-lined serving plate and spoon the held-over one-half melted candy-bars over top of puffs.

BONUS: If you don't own a pastry bag, you can make small mounds of dough with a teaspoon.

BLARNEY STONES

These Blarney Stones are akin to petit fours—but with added texture and decor...

2 cups granulated sugar
2 cups cake flour
1 cup hot water
1 tablespoon instant coffee
powder (optional)

If using coffee powder—mix with hot water—then add the water to the sugar and cake flour and hold overnight.

Next day:

5 egg whites—stiffly beaten
1 teaspoon cream of tartar
2 teaspoons baking powder
Pinch of salt
1 teaspoon vanilla

Fold the egg white mixture into the sugar-flour mixture.

Pour into a greased and floured jelly-roll-cookie sheet (17x12x2-inches).

Bake at 350 degrees for 30 minutes.

Let cool and cut in long narrow strips and then rectangles (about 2 inches long and 1½ inches wide).

Frost on all sides and roll in crushed peanuts.

FROSTING:

1—4 ounce package cream
cheese
1 stick margarine—room
temperature
2½ cups powdered sugar
1 teaspoon vanilla
Dash of salt

Mix until soft and creamy; frost the bars and then roll in crushed or finely chopped peanuts (Planters Cocktail peanuts are good as are ground Spanish Peanuts).

BONUS: If you freeze the bars first—they are easier to handle for frosting—then can be stored in freezer again. The bars are very good without the coffee—I prefer them *pure as the driven snow.*

BRANDY SNAP CORNUCOPIAS

An impressive finale to a sumptuous dinner!

¼ cup butter
3 tablespoons light corn
  syrup (Karo)
2 tablespoons sugar
2 tablespoons light molasses
½ cup all-purpose flour
2 teaspoons brandy
½ teaspoon ground ginger

Heat butter, corn syrup, sugar and molasses in top of double boiler over simmering water, stirring constantly until sugar dissolves and mixture is smooth.

Remove from heat and stir in the flour, brandy and ginger until smooth.

Drop by rounded teaspoon about 4 inches apart onto a well-buttered cookie sheet. Don't try to make more than four at one time.

Bake in a 350 degree oven until cookies spread into 3 to 4-inch circles and turn golden—about 5 minutes.

Remove from oven and cool oh-so-slightly—just until edge is firm enough to lift off with a spatula. Quickly roll on handle of a wooden spoon into the shape of a cornucopia.

After completely cooled fill with Brandy Whipped Cream.

**BRANDY WHIPPED
CREAM:**

1 cup whipping cream
¼ cup powdered sugar
2 teaspoons brandy

Whip the cream, adding the powdered sugar and brandy. Before serving pipe whipped cream into the cornucopias and refrigerate.

Yield: About 24

BONUS: I make the Brandy Cornucopias up ahead of time, fill

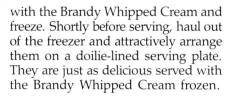

with the Brandy Whipped Cream and freeze. Shortly before serving, haul out of the freezer and attractively arrange them on a doilie-lined serving plate. They are just as delicious served with the Brandy Whipped Cream frozen.

ENGLISH TOFFEE BARS

Unbelievably simplistic and delicious!

15 graham crackers
(2½ x 2 ½-inch)
1 cup firmly packed brown
sugar
1 cup butter
(do not substitute)
1—6-ounce package
chocolate chips (Nestle's
milk chocolate)
¼ cups chopped nuts
(do not omit)

In a foil-lined 13x9-inch cake pan (grease the foil with butter), arrange the graham crackers. Entire bottom of pan must be covered with graham crackers—you might have to break to make an even fit.

In medium saucepan, combine the brown sugar and butter and bring to a boil.
Remove from heat—pour over graham crackers.

Bake in 400 degree oven for 5 minutes. Remove and immediately sprinkle with chocolate chips and as soon as the chips are soft, spread over the top of the cracker crust. Sprinkle with nuts. Chill at least 30 minutes or until chocolate is set. Break into pieces of all shapes and sizes (like English Toffee candy).

Store covered in refrigerator.

Yield: At least 24 bits and pieces.

BONUS: Guaranteed there will be nothing left to freeze, but if you should make a batch just for that purpose—the cookies do this nicely.

ORANGE-SLICE DATE BARS

Innovative are these date bars. If you like the combination of dates and oranges—you've hit the jackpot. Try these soon!

FILLING:

½ **pound dates, chopped**
1 cup water
½ **cup granulated sugar**
2 tablespoons flour

Combine in saucepan and cook until thickened and dates soften—10-15 minutes. COOL.

BATTER:

¾ **cup shortening**
1 cup brown sugar
2 eggs
1 teaspoon soda
  in 2 tablespoons hot water
1 teaspoon vanilla
1¾ **cups all-purpose flour**
¼ **teaspoon salt**
½ **cup nuts, finely chopped**
1—15 ounce package orange
  candy orange slices (cut
  in third's)

Cream the shortening and sugar. Blend in eggs; add soda mixture, and vanilla. Stir in the flour, and salt.

Spread one-half of the batter in a greased and floured 9x13-inch pan. Cover with orange slices (which have been cut in third's), sprinkle with nuts; spread the date filling over the orange slices and nuts; top with remaining batter.

Bake in 350 degree oven for 40 minutes. Remove, cool and cut into desired-size bars.

BONUS: You should have a pan layered thusly:
1. One-half of the batter.
2. Orange candy slices (cut in third's).
3. Nuts.
4. Date filling.
5. One-half of the batter.

PINEAPPLE BARS

DO NOT PASS UP—the recipe may be unpretentious, but these delicious bars will disappear quicker than a wink.

2¼ cups Graham cracker crumbs
½ cup melted butter

Mix the crumbs and butter together and press into an 8x12-inch pan. Bake in 250 degree oven for 20 minutes. Cool.

½ cup butter, room temperature
1½ cups powdered sugar
2 eggs (unbeaten)
1 cup crushed pineapple— well drained
1 cup whipping cream

Cream the butter and sugar, add eggs. Beat until stiff. Spread over the cooled crumb layer.

Whip cream and add pineapple. Spread this mixture over butter-sugar-egg layer. Sprinkle with Graham cracker crumbs (approximately ½ cup) and chill at least 5 hours.

Cut and serve.

PEG'S PEANUT BUTTER BARS

*An easy-put-together Peanut Butter Bar—enjoyed by both genders - young and **olders**...*

FIRST LAYER:

1 cup all-purpose flour
½ cup granulated sugar
½ cup margarine

Mix together. Line bottom of 9x13-inch cake pan with First Layer and bake 7—10 minutes in 350 degee oven. Remove from oven and turn oven to 425 degrees.

SECOND LAYER:

⅔ cup melted shortening
4 cups Quick Quaker Oats

Pour melted shortening over oatmeal and combine. Add remaining ingre-

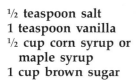
½ teaspoon salt
1 teaspoon vanilla
½ cup corn syrup or
    maple syrup
1 cup brown sugar

dients and pour over FIRST LAYER. Bake for 10 minutes in 425 degree oven. Remove from oven and cool.

THIRD LAYER:

⅔ cup peanut butter
    (creamy or crunchy)
1—12 ounce package
    chocolate chips

Melt together in saucepan over medium heat. When FIRST AND SECOND LAYER is cooled, pour the melted peanut butter and chocolate chips over them and spread evenly.

Refrigerate until solid. Cut in squares before serving.

BONUS: This makes a large batch—so if there are by some miracle a few left over—wrap and freeze. Beware—they are addictive.

GRAM GRADY'S DATE PIN WHEELS

*Surely, everyone has tasted date pinwheel cookies—if you have missed out somewhere along the way, Gram Grady's are the ones you will want to make, taste—and then hide some for your morning coffee break—these yummies will be speedily **eaten alive.***

FILLING:

1 cup granulated sugar
1 cup water
1 cup chopped nuts
2¼ cups chopped dates

Cook the filling in a saucepan until dates are softened (about 10 minutes).

DOUGH:

1 cup shortening
2 cups brown sugar
3 eggs

Mix ingredients well. Chill the dough (overnight is best). Divide dough in three parts, then roll to ¼ inch

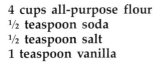
4 cups all-purpose flour
½ teaspoon soda
½ teaspoon salt
1 teaspoon vanilla

thickness. Spread with the date filling. Roll as for a Jelly Roll. Chill again. Slice 3/8-inch thick. Place on lightly greased cookie sheet.

Bake at 375 degrees for 8—10 minutes.

BONUS: The Pin Wheels freeze nicely. Keep in air-tight container if you want them *ready and waiting* for immediate consumption.

OATMEAL CRUNCHIES

Oatmeal cookies with a different approach. These yummies are dipped in sugar before baking.

1 cup all-purpose flour
½ cup granulated sugar
½ teaspoon baking powder
½ teaspoon baking soda
¼ teaspoon salt
½ cup brown sugar
½ cup solid vegetable
  shortening
1 egg
1 teaspoon vanilla
¾ cup quick-cooking rolled
  oats
¼ cup chopped walnuts

In a large mixer bowl, combine brown sugar, shortening, egg and vanilla—beat well on medium speed.

Sift together the flour, granulated sugar, baking powder, soda, and salt. Blend into the first mixture. Stir in rolled oats and walnuts.

Form dough into small balls (approximately 1 rounded teaspoon). Dip tops in additional granulated sugar. Place about 1½ inches apart on ungreased cookie sheet.

Bake in 375 degree oven for 10—12 minutes, until just golden. Remove from cookie sheet to rack for cooling.

Yield: 3½ dozen cookies.

UNSURPASSABLE CHOCOLATE CHIP COOKIES

Absolutely unsurpassable—these chocolate chip cookies are like none you have ever tasted. Unless you are prepared to eat more than you should—DO NOT EAT THEM WARM FROM THE OVEN— you will become an immediate Unsurpassable addict.

1 cup butter
1½ cups packed light
  brown sugar
1 egg
2 teaspoons vanilla
2 cups all-purpose flour
1 teaspoon baking soda
1 teaspoon cinnamon
1 teaspoon ground ginger
½ teaspoon salt

1—12 ounce package
  semisweet chocolate chips
1 cup chopped nuts—pecans
  or walnuts

1 cup powdered sugar

With an electric mixer, cream the butter, adding the brown sugar, egg and vanilla.

Combine the flour, baking soda, ginger, salt and cinnamon. Blend into the butter mixture. Stir in the chocolate chips and nuts. Chill until firm. Can be refrigerated overnight.

Between palms of hands, roll small pieces of dough (scant teaspoon) into 1-inch rounds and dredge in powdered sugar. Place on lightly greased cookie sheets—about 2 inches apart.

Bake in 375 degree oven for 10 minutes. Remove from oven, cool 5 minutes on cookie sheets before removing to racks. Store in airtight container.

Yield: 6 dozen

BUTTER SUGAR COOKIES

*Of the very many sugar cookie recipes given to me, this one is truly the Best. Men especially like them. These cookies are deceivingly **plain**, but utterly melt in your mouth.*

**1 cup butter
(DO NOT USE
MARGARINE)
½ cup granulated sugar
½ cup powdered sugar
1 egg
2 cups plus 2 tablespoons
all-purpose flour
½ teaspoon cream of tartar
½ teaspoon baking soda
2 teaspoons vanilla**

Cream together the butter, sugars and egg. Gradually mix in the dry ingredients and vanilla.

Roll into small balls (rounded teaspoonful of dough), place about 2 inches apart on ungreased cookie sheet; dip bottom of a buttered glass in granulated sugar and press down to form cookies. Use a cookie press if you have one, but the glass works fine.

Bake in 375 degree oven for 10–12 minutes. Do not let them get brown.

Remove cookies to racks and cool before adding to the cookie jar.

Yield: 3 dozen

BONUS: Great freezer cookies.

HOMEMADE LADYFINGERS

*If you are lucky enough to live in a city where the **local bakeries** provide ladyfingers daily—you probably won't be interested in this recipe—but for those of us who cannot locate ladyfingers in our local baking establishments—the following recipe is quite unassuming and provides delicious ladyfingers **by homemade**.*

4 egg whites
Dash of salt
¼ cup granulated sugar

Beat the egg whites and salt in large mixer bowl until soft peaks form (peaks will *curl*); then gradually add ¼ cup granulated sugar until stiff peaks form (peaks stand straight).

4 egg yolks
¼ cup granulated sugar
2 teaspoons lemon juice
1 teaspoon vanilla

In small mixer bowl, beat the egg yolks until foamy; gradually add ¼ cup sugar and beat until thick and lemon-colored. Beat in lemon juice and vanilla.

Fold the yolk mixture into the egg white mixture.

¾ cup sifted cake flour

FOLD the sifted cake flour into the egg mixture.

Line a baking sheet with plain brown paper; insert a straight-sided ½ inch round tip in a pastry bag; fill with batter.
Pipe 1x3-inch strips 1 inch apart on paper. Lightly sprinkle sifted powdered sugar atop the ladyfingers.

Bake in 350 degree oven for 8—10 minutes. Remove from oven and cool on rack.

Yield: Approximately 6 dozen.

BONUS: If you have any ladyfingers left over from the incumbent dessert at hand—freeze for future dessert developments...

SALLY'S ALMOND LACE WAFERS

Almond Lace Wafers bespeak themselves—an excellent old family recipe from a dear friend of mine—a batch of these lacy wafers will disappear in record time.

¾ cup finely ground
   almonds (a food processor
   is great for this)
½ cup butter
   (don't substitute)
1 tablespoon cream
1 tablespoon flour
½ cup granulated sugar

Combine all ingredients in a small saucepan. Heat over low heat, stirring constantly until the butter melts.
Drop by heaping teaspoon on a well buttered and floured cookie sheet (Sally says she has better luck with a pan).

Only do four cookies at a time.

Bake at 350 degrees about 4—5 minutes or until light brown and still bubbly in the center. Remove from oven and let cool on sheet just until edge is firm enough to lift with a spatula. Put top side down on paper towel and quickly roll on handle of a wooden spoon.

Wipe cookie sheet each time with a paper towel and reflour.

Yield: About 2 dozen

SALTED NUT ROLL SQUARES

*Reminiscent of that favorite salted nut roll—the delight of many. These nut roll squares are remindful of those **nut roll breaks**.*

1½ cups all-purpose flour
½ cup firmly packed brown sugar
½ teaspoon baking powder
½ teaspoon salt
¼ teaspoon baking soda
½ cup butter, softened
1 teaspoon vanilla
2 egg yolks

3 cups miniature marshmallows

TOPPING:
⅔ cup corn syrup
¼ cup butter
2 teaspoons vanilla
1—12-ounce package peanut butter chips (Nestle's)
2 cups crispy rice cereal (Rice Krispies)
2 cups peanuts (Planter's cocktail peanuts)

In large bowl, combine the crust ingredients (flour, sugar, etc.)— hold out the marshmallows.

Press the crumb mixture in bottom of an ungreased 9x13-inch pan. Bake in 350 degree oven until light golden brown—12—15 minutes. Remove from oven and immediately spoon marshmallows evenly on top of crust. Return to oven for at least 2 minutes or until marshmallows begin to puff. Remove from oven and cool.

In large sauce pan, heat corn syrup, butter, vanilla and peanut butter chips just until chips melt—stir mixture to smooth texture. Remove from heat, stir in the cereal and peanuts. Spoon warm topping over the marshmallows and spread to cover evenly. Chill and cut into 36 bars.

BONUS: These bars *travel* well—and are good mailers, too. I have also frozen them successfully.

ETC.:

ETC.:

INSTANT WHITE SAUCE MIX

Absolutely the best white sauce mix—instant or otherwise. Just mix up a batch and keep a jar of it handy in the refrigerator.

2²/₃ cup powdered milk
  (or buttermilk)
1 cup butter or margarine
1½ cups all-purpose flour
2 teaspoons salt

Blend ingredients with pastry blender or in blender until they become consistency of granulated sugar. Keep in covered jar in refrigerator. To make one cup of white sauce, add 1 cup water to ½ cup mix.

BLENDER BEARNAISE SAUCE

A never-fail, no-cook, Bearnaise Sauce that you will use frequently - it is spectacular.

6 green onions or shallots,
  minced
¼ cup wine vinegar
4 egg yolks
2 teaspoons dried tarragon
¼ teaspoon salt
¼ teaspoon dry mustard
Dash Tabasco
1 cup melted butter

Cook the onions in wine vinegar until liquid is absorbed and the onion tender. Put in blender with egg yolks, dried tarragon, salt, dry mustard and Tabasco. Blend for 5 seconds, gradually adding the melted butter.

Sauce will thicken at once. If too thick, a small amount of hot water may be added.

HOLLANDAISE SAUCE

2 egg yolks
½ cup butter—divided
  into thirds
1 tablespoon fresh lemon
  juice

Combine the egg yolks and lemon juice in top of double boiler over hot but not boiling water. Add the butter one-third at a time, constantly stirring until completely melted. Continue stirring until sauce thickens.

BUTTERSCOTCH SAUCE

A splendid topping for that one scoop of vanilla ice cream.

1¼ **cups brown sugar**
⅔ **cup dark corn syrup**
   (Karo)
4 **tablespoons butter**
½ **cup thick cream**
¼ **cup milk**

Mix the brown sugar, syrup and butter. Bring to a boil and cook to soft ball stage. Remove from heat, add the cream and milk.

Cool before serving so it doesn't melt the ice cream.

HONEY BUNCH SYRUP

Another delectable topping for ice cream.

½ **cup brown sugar**
½ **cup light syrup (Karo)**
½ **cup whipping cream**

Boil until you can lift a spoonful out and there are no bubbles in the syrup.

Cool before serving.

KAHLUA VELVET BLIZZARD

Unusually smooth and refreshing. Kahlua Velvet Blizzard is a fantastic way to end an evening.

1 **quart vanilla ice cream—**
   softened
4 **ounces Kahlua**
2 **ounces Creme de Cacao**
½ **half cup thick cream**

Blend all ingredients well. Pour into parfaits or tall, slim glasses. Freeze.

Serve directly from freezer.

Yield: Depending on size of glasses—8—10

BLOODY MARY MIX

This is a superb means of using up all of those summer tomatoes so you can enjoy them throughout the winter months.

9 pounds tomatoes
   (approximately 30
   medium size)
¼ cup fresh lemon juice
2 tablespoons Worcestershire
   sauce
1 tablespoon celery salt
2 teaspoons salt
1 teaspoon onion powder
½ teaspoon bottled hot
   pepper sauce
¼ teaspoon pepper
¼ teaspoon cayenne

Skin the tomatoes; removing stem ends and cores. Quarter the tomatoes into a 10-quart kettle or Dutch oven. Slowly cook the tomatoes covered, 15 minutes or till soft. Stir often to prevent sticking.

Press the tomatoes through a food mill to extract juice (or use your food processor and pour through strainer to collect any seeds)— measure 12 cups juice. Return to kettle; stir in the lemon juice and all other seasonings. Bring mixture to boiling and boil 2 minutes.

Pour hot juice into clean, hot canning jars leaving a half inch headspace. Seal with lids as per manufacturer's instructions. Process in boiling water bath—10 minutes for pints, 15 minutes for quarts.

Yield: 6 pints or 3 quarts

Use as for any Bloody Mary you would normally *build*. For a Virgin Mary Cocktail (non-alcoholic) pour over ice and serve. It's fun to garnish with a couple of giant stuffed green olives on a pick instead of a celery stick which without fail is cumbersome and no one knows quite how to rid themselves of it.

HOT BUTTERED RUM MIX

Less expensive and excitingly warms the cockles of one's heart!

1 pound unsalted butter (room temperature)
2 pounds (5 cups) packed brown sugar
2 tablespoons ground cinnamon
1 teaspoon freshly ground nutmeg
1 teaspoon vanilla extract

Mix the softened butter and brown sugar, cinnamon, freshly ground nutmeg and vanilla together. Refrigerate or freeze.

For each serving, use 1 tablespoon of the mix, 1½ ounces dark rum and 6 ounces boiling water.

BONUS: If someone prefers a hot whiskey, use whiskey in place of the rum. This mix freezes indefinitely; I have also kept the mix refrigerated for at least six months without spoiling. It is an excellent *keeper* and great to have at a moment's notice.

MAGIC CRABAPPLE JUICE

Not unlike magic, if you live in an area where crabapples grow handily in your backyard—or your neighbor's—try this juice for a most pleasant surprise.

5 quarts water
1—2-ounce can Cream of Tartar
3 quarts crabapples
1 cup sugar (or more—depending on crabapples)

Boil together the water and Cream of Tartar.

Add the apples and hold aside for 24 hours.

Next day, drain apples through a nylon.

Add sugar and re-boil until sugar is dissolved.

Pour into jars and refrigerate or seal if to be kept on shelf.

VANILLA, ABOVE & BEYOND

If you enjoy the taste of vanilla, you certainly won't have trouble finding recipes that call for it, but have you dared to experiment with the Vanilla bean itself? Try making your own vanilla extract by adding two split vanilla beans to 1 cup of cognac or vodka in a sterilized glass container. Cover and forget about it for at least two months.

For a pistachio flavor in cakes, sauces or quick sweet breads or yeast breads, add ½ teaspoon vanilla and ½ teaspoon almond extract.

Make vanilla sugar by placing a dried vanilla bean (after you have used it a couple of times for flavoring) with 1 cup fine granulated sugar into a blender jar; cover and blend on high speed until bean is completely pulverized. Strain the sugar through a fine sieve and store in a covered glass container.

Vanilla sugar is utterly fantastic used to sweeten whipped cream, cinnamon toast or sprinkled vicariously over fresh fruits and topped with fresh grated nutmeg.

Dare to be unconventional and come up with your own imaginative ideas for the fabulous Vanilla Bean.

ECHO LAKE TURKEY DRESSING

The ultimate in stuffings. Try this on your next turkey-stuffing project—and don't wait until Thanksgiving.

2—14 ½-ounce cans clear
  chicken broth
3 pounds bulk sausage
2 packages stuffing croutons
2—8-ounce packages slivered
  almonds
1 pound fresh mushrooms—
  sliced
1—8-ounce package
  sunflower seeds
3 stalks celery, chopped
2 tablespoons onion flakes
Season generously with
  Alpine Touch seasoning
  and grated parmesan
  cheese. (If Alpine Touch
  is not available in your
  area, use any brand
  Seasoned Salt).

In 4 tablespoons butter, saute the mushrooms, almonds, sunflower seeds, celery and onion. Brown the sausage.

Mix all ingredients together. Hold overnight in refrigerator.

This makes enough to stuff a 25-pound turkey.

BONUS: If you like a *wetter* dressing, add more chicken broth or chicken bouillon. Don't be afraid to be generous with the parmesan cheese.

TORTILLA BREAD

Good served with your favorite Mexican hot-dish.

1½ sticks butter,
  room temperature
1 teaspoon cumin
2 dozen flour tortillas

Mix the butter and cumin together to spreading consistency.

Spread mixture over entire surface of each tortilla and stack 12 on a piece of foil. Heat in 325 degree oven about 10 minutes.

Remove when warmed and roll each tortilla, jelly-roll fashion and serve as bread.

BUTTER CARAMELS

2 cups heavy cream
4 ounces sweetened
   condensed milk
2 cups granulated sugar
2 cups Karo light corn syrup
½ cup butter
   (do not substitute)
1 tablespoon vanilla

Combine the sugar, syrup, butter and one cup of the heavy cream in heavy large saucepan. With a wooden spoon continue stirring until butter is melted and mixture comes to a full boil. At this point slowly add the remaining one cup of heavy cream and the 4 ounces condensed milk, in a steady stream—not all at once. Continue stirring during this stage. The mixture should continue to boil while adding the cream slowly. After cream is added, turn heat to medium so that caramel mixture continues cooking at a slow boil. Cook for about 1 hour or until firm, soft ball is formed in cold water or 230 degrees on your candy thermometer.

Remove from heat, stir in vanilla and pour into 9x13 inch buttered Pyrex dish or shallow pan. Let cool to set. Cut into desired squares and wrap individually.

Yield: 2 pounds

BONUS: Remember not to attempt candy making on a cloudy, wet, humid day. It will remain sticky and not reach that 230 degree *setting* stage. I find this particularly true with caramels, divinity or almond roca.

CHOCOLATE FUDGE PECANS

A quick and easy treat for a rainy afternoon or to take along as a hostess gift.

½ **cup butter**
¾ **cup brown sugar**

Stir together in a small saucepan over low heat for 7 minutes.

In a 9x9-inch buttered pan, layer pecans. Pour mixture over the nuts and then disperse a 6-ounce package of chocolate chips over all. Cover the pan so chips will melt—with a small spatula or knife swirl the melted chocolate chips over the nut mixture. Refrigerate to set.

FRUITCAKE SUPREME

*Most generally, I would pass up a recipe for fruitcake. However, this almost **cakeless** fruitcake is truly supreme and deserves a special spot in ETC. of **BEST OF FRIENDS, ETC.***

1½ **cups whole Brazil nuts**
1½ **cups walnut halves**
1—8-ounce **package pitted dates**
½ **cup whole candied red maraschino cherries**
1⅓ **cups green and yellow candied pineapple rings, cut into chunks**
¾ **cup all-purpose flour**
1 **cup sugar**
½ **teaspoon salt**
½ **teaspoon baking powder**
3 **eggs**
1 **teaspoon vanilla**

DO NOT BREAK OR CUT ANY OF THE FRUITS AND NUTS UNLESS SPECIFIED. Place altogether in a large mixing bowl.

Combine the dry ingredients and sift over the fruit and nut mixture. Toss with your hands until ingredients are well coated with the dry mixture. Beat eggs until light. Add vanilla and blend. Pour this over the fruit mixture. Using a large wooden spoon, blend all ingredients in bowl.

Spoon into greased 9x5x2 ½-inch bread pans.

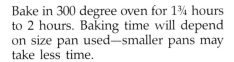

Bake in 300 degree oven for 1¾ hours to 2 hours. Baking time will depend on size pan used—smaller pans may take less time.

Yield: 2 to 3 cakes—depending on size of pan.

BONUS: Add a little brandy to baked cakes if you enjoy that extra little *oomph* - but certainly not a must. Cakes are better if given a chance to *ripen*. They can be stored in the freezer or refrigerator.

HOT BRANDIED PEACHES

A splendid accomplice with lunch, brunch or light one-dish dinners.

**2 large cans peach halves—
including juice (or fresh
if in season)
¾ cup light brown sugar
1 teaspoon pumpkin
pie spice
Rind of one-half lemon—
grated
2 tablespoons butter
½ cup brandy**

Place peaches in a shallow casserole. Pour juice over all. Sprinkle with the mixture of butter, brown sugar, spice, and lemon rind.
Place in 400 degree oven and bake until butter mixture liquifies and is bubbly.

Yield: 8—10 servings—depending on how many peach halves are in the cans.

BONUS: Serve warm as is or with a dollop of vanilla flavored whipped cream.

If you use fresh peaches (which rate a gold star in my humble opinion), just sprinkle with the butter-sugar mixture and continue. They won't be as *syrupy* but more carmelized.

FESTIVE POPCORN CAKE

The construction of this popcorn cake is only half the fun.. the other half is the consumption.

9 cups popped popcorn
1 cup miniature gumdrops
1 cup nuts (pecans are
  pleasurable)
½ cup crushed candy cane
  (or peppermint sticks)

8 cups miniature
  marshmallows
½ cup vegetable oil
½ cup margarine

Mix together the popped popcorn, gumdrops, nuts and candy cane.

In the top of a double boiler, melt the marshmallows, vegetable oil and margarine. Pour over the popcorn mixture and press into a 10-inch tube pan which has been lined with foil. Cool completely, unmold from pan, slice and enjoy!

HONEY & ORANGE POPCORN

With the addition of sunflower and pumpkin seeds, this popcorn treat becomes a nutritious snack.

5 quarts popped popcorn
½ cup shelled sunflower
  seeds
½ cup pumpkin seeds
½ cup melted butter
½ cup honey
1 tablespoon fresh grated
  orange peel
¼ teaspoon fresh grated
  nutmeg

Place the popped popcorn and seeds in a large roasting pan. Mix together the remaining ingredients and pour over the popcorn. Toss to mix well. Heat in a 300 degree oven for 15 minutes—stirring occasionally.

Yield: 5 quarts

LOW-CAL
PEANUT BUTTER POPCORN

If you're looking for a slender-snacking popcorn treat that is SCRUMPTIOUS BEYOND WORDS—head for the kitchen and get out the popper.

3 quarts popped popcorn (½ cup unpopped)
1 cup granulated sugar
½ cup honey
½ cup light corn syrup (Karo)
1 cup chunky peanut butter (or plain)
1 teaspoon vanilla

Keep popped popcorn in a large roasting pan in a warm 250 degree oven.

Butter sides of a heavy medium-size saucepan and mix together the sugar, honey and Karo syrup. Bring the mixture to a boil, stirring constantly. Boil hard for 2 minutes; remove from heat and stir in the peanut butter and vanilla.
Immediately pour over popcorn, stirring to coat well.

Cool and break into bite-size pieces (or eat it while just barely warm - it is superfluous).

Yield: 12 cups or 36 one-third cup snack servings—75 calories per serving.

BONUS: If you are not particularly interested in sparing the calories, add a cup of mixed nuts to the popped corn before pouring the syrup mixture over. The combination is DOUBLE SCRUMPTIOUS. If you have any uneaten morsels, store in air-tight container for the next *snacking-spree*.

SUGARED SPANISH PEANUTS

Addicting are these sugar glazed Spanish peanuts. You will have to hide these from yourself.

2 cups raw Spanish peanuts
  (with skins)
1 cup granulated sugar
½ cup water
Coarse ground salt

In heavy saucepan, combine the nuts, sugar and water. Place over medium-high heat. Cook and stir very carefully just until mixture crystallizes and coats the peanuts. This takes about 10 to 15 minutes - just until dry.

Spread peanuts on 15x15-inch cookie sheet. Sprinkle with coarse ground salt. Bake in 300 degree oven for 15 minutes turning once. Bake 15 minutes more.

Cool and store in covered container.

BONUS: Do not stir so much that the skins come off the peanuts—the skins are needed to hold the coating.

FIDDLESTIX

*An interestingly crunchy snack, relished by both masculine and feminine genders between the ages of **gummers** and **crunchers**.*

2 cups Spoon-size
  shredded wheat
2 cups miniature Pretzel
  twists or Pretzel sticks
2 cups mixed nuts
½ cup peanut crunchy
  peanut butter
½ cup butter
2 cups butterscotch morsels

Melt the peanut butter, butter and butterscotch morsels in top of a double boiler over simmering (not boiling) water. In the meantime, mix the shredded wheat, pretzels, and nuts in a large bowl. Pour the melted mixture over and mix with wooden spoon. Spread on a cookie sheet lined with waxpaper to *dry* . Store in covered container if you have any leftovers.

ORANGE SPICY NUTS

After you prepare these tempting orange glazed nuts, you will find it difficult not to have some on hand for all occasions — festive or not.

⅓ **cup granulated sugar**
½ **stick butter**
¼ **cup fresh orange juice**
1½ **teaspoons salt**
1¼ **teaspoons cinnamon**
¼ **teaspoon cayenne pepper**
¼ **teaspoon ground mace**
⅛ **teaspoon freshed grated nutmeg**

1 pound mixed nuts — i.e., pecans, macadamias, unblanched almonds, peanuts, walnuts, cashews.

Cook sugar, butter, orange juice and seasonings in large skillet or saucepan over low heat until butter melts and the sugar dissolves completely.

Increase heat to medium, add the nuts and toss until coated. Spread in a single layer on foil lined jelly roll pan.

Position rack in center of oven.

Bake 1 hour, at 250 degrees, stirring every 15 minutes.

REMOVE from oven and transfer nuts to large sheet of foil. Separate with fork. Cool completely and store in air-tight container.

BONUS: Can be frozen, or kept in refrigerator indefinitely. Bring to room temperature before serving. If sticky, warm in 250 degree oven about 10 minutes.

ALL-AMERICAN VANILLA ICE CREAM

An all-time favorite among ice cream lovers. It is special by itself and becomes extra special when served with Honey Bunch Syrup or Hot Fudge Sauce.

1½ cups granulated sugar
¼ cup flour
Dash of salt
2 cups milk
4 eggs, slightly beaten
1 quart heavy cream
2 tablespoons vanilla

Combine the sugar, flour and salt in a large saucepan and stir in the milk. Cook over medium heat, stirring constantly until mixture thickens and bubbles for 1 minute.

Stir half of the hot mixture slowly into the beaten eggs in a medium size bowl; stir back into the remaining hot mixture in the saucepan. cook, stirring for 1 minute.

Pour into a large bowl; blend in the heavy cream and vanilla. Chill at least 2 hours.

Pour mixture into prepared 4—6 quart freezer can and follow manufacturer's directions for making the ice cream.

Yield: Approximately 2 quarts

BONUS: If your freezer is smaller, freeze half the mixture at a time. Pack the ice cream in plastic containers; freeze until firm.

FISH AND CHIPS BATTER

2 cups all-purpose flour
5 teaspoons cornstarch
1½ teaspoons sugar
3 teaspoons salt
1 teaspoon baking powder
1 teaspoon baking soda

Blend together all of the above and whisk in enough cold water until consistency is that of a *slightly* thick pancake batter. One-half of the above recipe is enough for serving five or six persons.

BEER BATTER FOR SHRIMP

1 cup all-purpose flour
½ cup cornstarch
1 tablespoon baking powder
1 tablespoon salt
1 tablespoon seasoned salt
  or ACCENT
3 eggs
½ cup cold beer

Mix all of the above and whisk until well blended.

TEMPURA & TEMPURA SAUCE

Tempura, unlike other batters, is delicate and lacy thus distinguishing Tempura from most deep-fried foods. It should also be fried at a lower temperature. Shrimp, fresh mushrooms, fresh broccoli, onion rings and thin sliced potato wafers are only a few of the foods that excel as Tempura fare.

1 slightly beaten egg
1 cup iced water
1 cup all-purpose flour

In a medium mixing bowl, stir the egg and iced water together, adding flour all at once. Beat with a rotary beater until very smooth.

Use peanut oil or vegetable oil for cooking.

BONUS: TEMPURA SAUCE for dipping: Stir together in a small saucepan: 1 cup water, ¼ cup dry sherry, ¼ cup soy sauce, 1 teaspoon sugar and 1 teaspoon instant chicken bouillon granules or 1 bouillon cube. Cook and stir until boiling. Makes about 1 cup.

CHILI SAUCE

Better than any you can buy. Use up those end of the season tomatoes from the garden.

16 ripe tomatoes
12 big red bell peppers
3 small chile peppers
crushed
1 bud garlic
2 cups plus—white vinegar
1 tablespoon salt
1 tablespoon celery salt
1 tablespoon dry mustard
½ cup granulated sugar

Peel tomatoes and quarter. Grind the tomatoes and red bell peppers (or dust off that food processor and use steel blade to chop). In a large stock pot or roaster, add the ground tomatoes and peppers together with all other ingredients. Cook on low simmering heat for 2 hours.

Pour into hot sterilized jars, use cold pack processing method. (Or if you have refrigerator space, you can keep in refrigerator).

Yield—5 pints

BONUS: Use as you would in any recipes calling for chili sauce. It is delightful with scrambled eggs; mix a little horseradish with it for a Shrimp sauce.

SEAFOOD SALAD DRESSING

1½ cups chili sauce
¼ cup celery—
finely chopped
¼ cup dill pickles,
finely chopped
2 cups Low Cal Mayonnaise
1 teaspoon lemon juice
½ teaspoon Worcestershire
sauce
1 teaspoon horseradish

Put all ingredients into bowl, mix together until well blended—or run through a blender. Keep in cool place but not in refrigerator. It will keep indefinitely. Makes one quart.

KOSHER DILLS

A crispier, tastier, easier Kosher dill pickle does not exist. Allow one pound of pickling cucumbers per one-quart jar.

6 cups water
2 cups cider vinegar
⅓ cup pickling salt
(DO NOT USE IODIZED SALT)
Scant ¼ cup granulated sugar
Alum (¼ teaspoon per quart jar)

Garlic buds, red chilies, quartered white onions, (or small pickling onions), fresh dill.

Double the above water, vinegar, salt and sugar and bring to boil. The brine will fill 4 quarts. If your pan is large enough, triple the ingredients.

Into each jar put 1 garlic clove, 1 red chile, 1 quarter of onion (or 1 pickling onion), and pack the cucumbers (tightly) into the jars. Add the ¼ teaspoon alum to each jar, and on top of the pickles pack in a nice, fresh head of dill. Pour hot brine over all to cover the pickles (should fill at least quarter of an inch over the cukes).

Immediately seal with lids—following manufacturer's directions. I do not cold-pack or process my pickles but make certain the jars seal - test per instructions. Home economists insist the pickles should be water processed, but doing so softens them. I have been canning the Kosher Dills for over 25 years without processing as my mother has for at least 40 years—we are still alive and kicking, as are those who have partaken of the them. THE CHOICE IS YOURS.

BONUS: Use serving size, fresh-picked cucumbers (should be no more than one day old).

Also, if you prefer—you can omit the red chilies, but they give the pickles a little vigor.

HOLIDAY PEPPER JELLY

Make this tasty, gift-giving pepper jelly for a great hostess gift during the holidays; however, it is always welcomed any time of the year.

6 red bell peppers
6 green bell peppers

7 cups granulated sugar
1½ cups cider vinegar

1 bottle liquid pectin

Seed and julienne the peppers. In a large sauce pot, place the julienned peppers, sugar and vinegar. Boil for 1 minute. Empty in one bottle of liquid pectin and boil 3 minutes.

Remove from heat and ladle into hot sterilized jelly jars. Seal with melted paraffin.

Yield: 4 cups

SWEET POTATO RELISH

This relish is a savory buffet special served with ham, turkey, on any festive occasion.

1 pound sweet potatoes
3 tablespoons sweet
    pickle relish
1 bunch green onions,
    thinly sliced
½ cup finely diced celery
1/8 teaspoon freshly ground
    nutmeg
¼ teaspoon salt
1/8 teaspoon pepper
1 cup mayonnaise
    (more or less)
1 hard-boiled egg,
    finely diced

Boil the sweet potatoes in their skins, drain, peel and mash. To the potatoes add all other ingredients which have been combined.

SPICY-HOT PEACH CHUTNEY

BE PATIENT, AND AFTER AT LEAST TWO WEEKS, GIVE IT A TRY. IMPROVES WITH AGE. EAT MEASUREDLY AND DEFY THE MEDICINERS. A quote from the provider of this finest of chutneys.

1 medium green pepper, diced in small pieces
¼ cup fresh ginger root, grated
6 cloves of garlic, pressed, mashed or minced.
¼ cup hot chili peppers, minced (you may substitute 1 tablespoon cayenne pepper)

2 cups brown sugar (or 1 cup honey)
1 cup water (use a little less if you use honey instead of brown sugar)
2 cups cider vinegar
3 pounds fresh peaches, skinned, pitted and cut into small cubes
¾ cup raisins
1 tablespoon mustard seed
1 teaspoon coriander seed
1 teaspoon ground cloves (you may substitute ½ teaspoon cinnamon)

EXCEPT for the raisins and mustard seed, put all other ingredients into a pot. Bring to boil. Lower the heat and simmer for 30 minutes.

Add raisins and mustard seed to mixture in pot. Simmer for an additional 15 minutes, stirring often.

Pour into hot, sterilized, small canning jars and seal. Store.

Yield: 1 quart

DIVERSE BARBECUE SAUCE

2—14-ounce bottles ketchup
1—12-ounce bottle chili sauce
⅓ cup prepared mustard
1 tablespoon dry mustard
1½ cups firmly packed
  brown sugar
2 tablespoons coarse, freshly
  ground black pepper
1½ cups wine vinegar
1 cup fresh lemon juice
½ cup bottled thick steak
  sauce
Dash Tabasco or more
¼ cup Worcestershire
  sauce
1 tablespoon soy sauce
2 tablespoons salad oil
1—12-ounce can beer
1 clove garlic, minced
  or crushed (optional)

Combine all ingredients except the garlic and mix well. Pour into pint jars to store in refrigerator for several weeks or freeze for longer storage. About an hour before using the sauce, add the garlic, if desired.

Yield: About 6 pints

BONUS: Actually, the sauce will keep more than several weeks in the refrigerator. It does not seem to spoil any more than commercial sauces. Because of the sugar—which will burn if exposed to heat too long—this sauce is best added during the last third of cooking time. It should be somewhat toasted, or caramelized, however. Try it on oven-baked ribs or on bacon fried in a pan—the results are tasty.

WINTER SALAD

So nice to have on hand for those special winter-time festivities.

3 medium heads cabbage
6 large white onions
6 large carrots
1 green pepper
1 red pepper or if
  unavailable—a small jar of
  pimento

Shred all vegetables (use that food processor if you have one) and soak three hours in water to cover to which ¼ cup salt has been added. Drain well.

Mix together:

1 quart white vinegar
4—5 cups granulated sugar
1 tablespoon celery seed

Do not heat this mixture.

Pack the cabbage mixture loosely in

1 tablespoon mustard seed

jars. Cover with the cold vinegar mixture and seal.
(You do not have to use sterile process or cold pack). Marinate one week.

Yield: 5 or 6 quarts

BONUS: You can make half of this recipe—if you choose to do so, use ¾ recipe of the vinegar marinade. You can use any kind of jar for storing. I like to store in refrigerator.

FRESH PEACH JAM

You will be ecstatic to have this in your larder when the peach season is over.

4 cups peeled and finely
  chopped peaches
  (about 10 peaches)
2 tablespoons fresh lemon
  juice
½ teaspoon ground cloves
½ teaspoon ground allspice
½ teaspoon ground
  cinnamon
¼ teaspoon freshly grated
  nutmeg
5½ cups sugar
6 tablespoons (1 packet)
  liquid fruit pectin

In a large sauce pot, mix the peaches and spices. Bring to a boil and add sugar. Boil again for 1 minute. Remove from heat and stir in the pectin. Skim off any foam and pour into hot sterilized jars. Seal with paraffin.

Yield: 6 half pint jars

BONUS: To a few of the jars, add 1 tablespoon dark rum for a yummy ice cream topping.

HOLIDAY APRICOT JAM

*Holiday Apricot Jam is not exclusively for holiday giving. It is colorful, simple to make and for those of us who **adore** apricots, a **stupendous** treat any time of the year.*

3 cups chopped dried apricots
2 cups water
2 cups granulated sugar
2—8-ounce cans crushed pineapple (do not drain)
¾ cup maraschino cherries— drained and halved

In a heavy jelly cooking saucepan, combine apricots and water. Simmer for 8—10 minutes—until apricots are softened. Stir in the sugar and pineapple.

Bring mixture to a boil, reduce heat and simmer uncovered 45—60 minutes—or until mixture has thickened.

Stir cherry halves into apricot mixture; simmer 5 minutes longer.

Ladle into hot jars (which have been sterilized) leaving 1/8 inch at the top. Wipe rims of jars clean; place hot lids on jars and screw metal rings on firmly. Invert jars—then turn upright. Check for seal in 12 hours (as per manufacturer's instructions).

Yield: 5—6 8-ounce jars.

BONUS: This makes a nice hostess gift together with a loaf of freshly baked rolls or Honey Whole Wheat Bread.

RHUBARB-PLUS JELLY

*A terrific jelly that very nicely utilizes some of that **never-ending** rhubarb which either shows up at your front door like an unexpected guest or is growing profusely in your own backyard or passageway. Rhubarb jelly recipes are abundant, but this one has worked best for me—tastewise and ease in preparation.*

4 cups finely chopped rhubarb (food processor works super)
4 cups granulated sugar
1 15 ¼-ounce can crushed pineapple—DO NOT DRAIN
1 3-ounce package strawberry Jello

In a large sauce pot (Dutch oven works nicely) mix together the rhubarb, sugar and crushed pineapple. Cook over medium heat at a slow-rolling boil for 20 minutes. Stir occasionally.

Remove from heat and add the Jello, stirring to blend well. Pour into small jelly glasses (8-ounce are perfect)

Yield: 6—8-ounce jars.

BONUS: Cherry or raspberry flavored Jello are tasty alternatives. Also, I add ½ teaspoon *freshly grated nutmeg* - do this when you stir in the Jello.

CHOKECHERRY SYRUP

*The American College Dictionary describes the chokecherry as any of several species of cherry, especially PRUNUS VIRGINIANA of North America. I am most familiar with seeing it growing **wildly** along country roadsides, near creek beds and in lush little coulees in my native Montana and I remember it taking a **familial gathering** to pick enough of the astringent fruit to provide juice for concocting an energetic syrup for pancakes and the likes, or for a marvelously tart jelly.*

7 cups chokecherry juice
6 cups sugar

Wash the cherries and drain well. Place in an 8 to 10 quart kettle and add enough water to completely cover the cherries. Boil until tender—about 15 minutes, strain through a cloth *Jelly Bag*. Combine sugar and juice and bring to a boil. Boil rapidly for 20 to 25 minutes. Pour into hot, sterilized jars and seal.

BONUS: You can add liquid pectin to make chokecherry jelly. Follow instructions contained in pectin package.

WELSH RABBIT
(also known as WELSH RAREBIT)

The dictionary describes **Welsh Rabbit** *as melted cheese, usually mixed with ale, beer, milk, etc. and eaten on toast. There are definitely disparate, if not* **desperate** *rabbits on the horizon and the following is but one of them.*

2 tablespoons butter
16 ounces (4 cups) shredded
   sharp cheddar cheese
½ teaspoon Worcestershire
   sauce
½ teaspoon dry mustard
1/8 teaspoon Cayenne pepper
2 eggs—slightly beaten
½ cup half and half

2 English muffins, split,
   toasted and buttered
4 slices Canadian bacon
   (about ¼ inch thick)
4 slices tomato
   (about ¼ inch thick)

In a double boiler (or 2-quart saucepan) melt the butter; add cheese stirring constantly until cheese melts. Stir in the Worcestershire, mustard and Cayenne. Combine the eggs and half and half. Stir the egg mixture into the cheese mixture until well blended. Continue cooking until mixture thickens.

Assemble—placing one muffin half on each serving plate, top with a slice of hot Canadian bacon and a slice of tomato. Spoon the Rabbit (about ¼ cup) over each. Serve immediately while hot.

Yield—4 servings

BONUS: Double the Rabbit sauce and use 4 muffins to serve eight. Also, if you are not enthusiastic about serving tomatoes with hot cheese sauce, simply make sure you don't have any in the larder.

GENERAL INDEX

GENERAL INDEX
(Continued)

GENERAL INDEX
(Continued)